Ess

Paris

by
SUSAN GROSSMAN

Susan Grossman is a travel writer,
broadcaster and photographer, and is a
former travel editor of the Sunday Telegraph
Magazine. She has presented two series of
the BBC's 'Food and Drink' programme,
and has broadcast regularly on such radio
programmes as 'Breakaway'.

Produced by AA Publishing

Written by Susan Grossman
Peace and Quiet section
by Paul Sterry

Edited, designed and produced by AA
Publishing. Maps © The Automobile
Association 1994

Distributed in the United Kingdom by AA
Publishing, Fanum House, Basingstoke,
Hampshire, RG21 2EA.

The contents of this publication are believed
correct at the time of printing. Nevertheless,
the publishers cannot be held responsible
for any errors or omissions, or for changes
in details given in this guide or for the
consequences of any reliance on the
information provided by the same.
Assessments of attractions, hotels,
restaurants and so forth are based upon the
author's own experience and, therefore,
descriptions given in this guide necessarily
contain an element of subjective opinion
which may not reflect the publisher's
opinion or dictate a reader's own
experience on another occasion.
**We have tried to ensure accuracy in this
guide, but things do change and we
would be grateful if readers would advise
us of any inaccuracies they may
encounter.**

First published 1990
Revised Second Edition 1992
Revised Third Edition © The Automobile
Association 1994

A CIP catalogue record for this book is
available from the British Library.

ISBN 0 7495 0841 8

Published by AA Publishing, which is a
trading name of Automobile Association
Developments Limited, whose registered
office is Fanum House, Basingstoke,
Hampshire, RG21 2EA.
Registered number 1878835.

Colour separation: L. C. Repro & Sons,
Aldermaston

Printed by: Printers Trento, S.R.L., Italy

Front cover picture: *Pont d'Iéna and the
Tour Eiffel*

ACKNOWLEDGEMENTS
**The Automobile Association would like to thank
the following photographers and
libraries for their assistance in the compilation of
the book.**

SUSAN GROSSMAN18 Brasserie Lipp, 22/3 Musée
d'Orsay, 25 Picasso Museum, 68 Jo Goldenberg's
restaurant, 70/1 Pâtisserie, 72 Café de Flore, 74
Fanny's Tea Shop, 79 Breakfast Crillon Hotel, 80
Crillon Hotel, 82/3 Henry IV Hotel, 96 Kenzo's
Boutique, 102 Le Trumilou, 109 Bus, 121 La
Madeleine Church.

LANCASTER HOTEL 81 Lancaster Hotel

MARY EVANS PICTURE LIBRARY 9 Siege of the
Bastille

NATURE PHOTOGRAPHERS LTD 48 Beechwoods (B
Burbidge), 49 Crested Tit (M Gore), 50/1 Common
Violet (P Sterry), 53 Red Deer Stag (W S Paton)

BARRIE SMITH 4 Eiffel Tower, 8 Liberty, 11 The Left
Bank, 13 Paris Mime, 14/5 Place de la Concorde, 17
SNCF Train, 20 La Coupole, 21 the Louvre, 26 La
Géode, 27 Musée d'Art Moderne, 30 Arc de
Triomphe, 32/3 Notre-Dame Cathedral, 37 Parc de
Bagatelle, 46/7 Bois de Boulogne, 55 Les Halles
Forum, 56/7 Galeries Lafayette, 60 Place de la
Madeleine, 63 Animal Market, 65 Place St-Michel, 67
Terminus Nord Brasserie, 75 Cheese Shop, 77 & 78
Labels, 88 Seine by Night, 95 Place St Jacques, 97
Boy & Camera, 98/9 Musée d'Orsay, 100 Tuileries
Gardens, 103 Arc de Triomphe, 104 Traffic, 107
Lunch on Board, 114/5 Métro, 117 Eiffel Tower, 119
Musée d'Orsay, 122 Seine

ANTONY SOUTER (for AA Photo Library) 29 Musée
Rodin

SPECTRUM COLOUR LIBRARY 40/1 Parc Monceau,
42 Fontainebleau, 76 Cheese Stall, 78 Wine Tasting

ZEFA PICTURE LIBRARY UK LTD Cover Eiffel Tower,
5 Pompidou Centre, 6/7 Place du Tertre, 24 Sacré
Cœur, 44 Versailles, 85 Bâteau mouches, 86 Moulin
Rouge, 91 Lido, 92 Pigalle

Author's Acknowledgements
Susan Grossman wishes to thank the luxury Crillon
Hotel, 10 place de la Concorde, 8e; Tradotels, a
group of hotels in traditional buildings renovated to
3-star standards, Brymon Airways, and the French
Government Tourist Office for all the help they gave
in compiling this book.

This book employs a simple rating system to help choose which places to visit:

✓	'top ten'
♦♦♦	do not miss
♦♦	see if you can
♦	worth seeing if you have time

INTRODUCTION

The Eiffel Tower is Paris's best known monument, though less popular these days than Beaubourg. At 1,007 feet (307m), it was the tallest building in the world when it was constructed in 1889. Made of a latticework of pig iron, it has three platforms and 1,710 steps to the top, though the weary can take a lift. On a clear day you can see for 45 miles (72km)

INTRODUCTION

Paris is still one of the most romantic, chic and culturally rewarding cities in the world. Nowhere is there such a concentration of quality. You can drool over the exquisite displays of food, chocolates and fashion in the shop windows, and over menus outside restaurants perpetually full of a nation who take eating out almost as seriously as anything else and while you *can* spend the earth on anything from an *haute couture* costume to a gourmet meal, Paris can be remarkably good value for money.

The city is quite small and most of the main sites are within walking distance of each other. You cannot miss the main landmarks: the Eiffel Tower, the Arc de Triomphe and the Notre-Dame Cathedral, Beaubourg, the Louvre, and the new Musée d'Orsay. But if you are planning a long weekend it might be an idea to make Friday rather than Monday the additional day, as many museums and some shops shut at the beginning of the week. It is also worth remembering that some museums are free or cheaper on Sunday.

As for *gay Paris,* unlike many other cities, Paris does not close down at midnight. Brasseries stay open until the early hours, and you can dance, visit a cabaret or listen to jazz in a smoky basement until the dustcarts shatter the silence of the early morning streets.

The controversial Georges Pompidou Centre, or Beaubourg, houses the National Museum of Modern Art, as well as changing exhibitions. Designed by Richard Rogers and Renzo Piano its 'inside out' appearance has offended many although it certainly pulls in the crowds. Take the escalator up the outside for splendid views of the capital or take advantage of the free shows in the piazza outside

New Paris

If you have not been to Paris for a while you will find quite a few changes, many of them thanks to an enormous injection of money from President Mitterand to build new monuments and transform old ones. He is not, of course, the first President of France to want to leave his mark on the face of Paris. De Gaulle was responsible for the modern skyline of La Défense to the west of Paris and Pompidou for Paris's number one tourist attraction, Beaubourg, that bears his name. In the mid-1970s the 59-storey Montparnasse Tower on the Left Bank sprang up. Next came the exodus of Les Halles market, and the redevelopment of the whole site with the underground Forum des Halles shopping centre and the Georges Pompidou National Centre of Art and Culture.

The place du Tertre in Montmartre is where to go to get your portrait etched or sketched – for a price. The highest point in the capital, at 425ft (130m), Montmartre is topped by the icing- sugar dome of the Sacré Cœur Cathedral from which there are splendid views, especially at night

In the last few years another major museum, the Cité des Sciences et de l'Industrie, has opened on the site of the slaughterhouses at La Villette in the northeast of Paris, some 15 minutes by Métro from the centre. Refrigerated lorries had rendered the abattoirs obsolete, so the whole area has been turned into a *parc* (still to be completed) and science museum designed to help young people 'discover' for themselves through an impressive range of computers, machinery and hands-on exhibits. The complex, which also includes an enormous mirrored dome, La Géode, containing a revolutionary 180-degree cinema, already ranks as one of the capital's major attractions even if the majority of instructions to everything are in French only!

The Louvre is also undergoing change on a large scale. Underground excavations are creating space for major exhibits, and the opening of the Richelieu wing (previously home to the ministry of Finance) in 1993 gave the Louvre the distinction of being the world's largest museum, with work scheduled to continue until 1996.

Paris's collection of Impressionist paintings has been removed from the Jeu de Paume and

other galleries and now sits in splendour on the top floor of the new Musée d'Orsay on the Left Bank, the former Gare d'Orsay railway station converted into a magnificent national art gallery.

Other new landmarks include a surrealist 350-foot (107m) high marble Grande Arch at La Défense (offices, with a lift to the top to admire the view), and the modern Institut du Monde Arabe on the Left Bank, its windows made up of lenses which open and shut with the light. Chirac's huge Palais Omnisport centre for concerts and sporting events is at Bercy and Euro Disney has arrived amid much hyperbole in Marne La Vallée, the new town in the suburbs. Several areas of Paris have undergone a marked transformation, the Marais and the Bastille on the Right Bank in particular. The new opera house for the 'people', at the Bastille, is responsible for the changes there and was inaugurated on 13 July 1989, appropriately enough the eve of Bastille Day. The old Opéra, Opéra de Paris-Garnier, is now only used for ballet.

Many of the once derelict *hôtels* (mansions) of the Marais have been smartened up to house offices, restaurants, shops and the new Picasso Museum. Even the historic place des Vosges has been re-landscaped. Over recent years both these areas have taken on some of the character of the *sixième arrondissement* (sixth district), with art galleries, designer showrooms, jazz clubs and restaurants effectively extending the 'arty' side of Paris over the Seine onto the Right Bank.

Like any city, Paris has its down side. There are neons and a McDonalds on the Champs-Elysées, the Latin Quarter is packed with ethnic take-aways and a seedy nightlife prevails in Pigalle, behind Beaubourg, and near Montparnasse.

Old Paris

But what of the old Paris? You needn't worry. Lovers still walk arm in arm in the Luxembourg gardens and along the Seine. The glass-topped boats chug up and down the river, you can climb the Eiffel Tower, or have your portrait sketched in Montmartre's place du Tertre. The

girls at the Moulin Rouge and the Lido can-can
the night away, while outside the traffic jams up
the Champs-Elysées, and races round the
place de la Concorde and the Arc de
Triomphe as though every driver was on his
way to Le Mans. As for the women, young and
old, Left Bank or Right, they are still the most
elegant in the world.

History
Paris is dominated by the Seine which curves
through the centre. Along its banks you will
find Paris's most splendid architecture: Notre-
Dame Cathedral and the Sainte-Chapelle on
the Ile de la Cité, where Paris began, as well as
the magnificent Louvre Museum and the Eiffel
Tower, the symbol of France itself. The city has
had a chequered and bloody history, passing
from hand to hand over the centuries.

*Most of Paris's
monuments – old
and new – are
visible from the
Seine*

In the 3rd century BC a Gallic tribe made the Ile
de la Cité their fortified capital. In 52BC
Caesar's Roman legions called it Lutetia and
turned it into an important Roman centre, its

name being changed to Paris in AD360.
In the Early Middle Ages after the Romans had
left, several invasions threatened the
civilisation of the city – one by Attila the Hun,
though it did not succeed, another by the
Franks. During the famine that followed a
young woman called Geneviève helped the
people and eventually became the patron saint
of Paris.
The city was continuously in difficulty with the
Norman sieges, and the Hundred Years' War
stunted any real development until the time of the

Anon. Revolution. Trouble began on the morning of 14 July 1789 when a militant mob advanced on Les Invalides looking for weapons. They helped themselves to 28,000 rifles and headed for the Bastille where in a symbolic gesture, depicted above, they released all seven prisoners they found there. Bastille Day is celebrated every year with military bands and fireworks

Capetien monarchs. Then came the building of Notre-Dame in 1108, the building of the fortress of the Louvre in 1180 and the establishment of the Sorbonne university in 1285.

Through the reigns of François I, Catherine de Medici, and Henri III Paris grew, though there were bloody conflicts between Catholics and Protestants. But it was not until the 17th century, and in particular the reign of the Sun King Louis XIV, that Paris really blossomed. Versailles became his Royal Court and Les Invalides, Gobelins, the Louvre colonnade and the Comédie-Française were built. He abolished the municipality and Paris became ruled by the State.

By Louis XV's reign the crown was growing steadily more unpopular, there were disastrous overseas wars and financial problems at home although more buildings, the Panthéon, the Palais-Bourbon and the place de la Concorde were completed. Then came the Revolution that changed everything.

On 14 July, 1789 an angry mob stormed the Bastille and symbolically freed the prisoners and France from the aristocratic State. In 1792 Louis XVI and his queen, Marie Antoinette, were imprisoned, and a year later they were executed. A Reign of Terror followed where

2,800 people in Paris lost their heads, ending with Napoleon appointing himself the new dictator in 1799. From then on Paris became prosperous. But in 1814 Paris fell to the invading allied armies and Napoleon was exiled and fought his last battle at Waterloo. During the Restoration in the 1840s, the Thiers fortifications were built round the city, forming the boundary of the present Périphérique (ring road).

In the 19th century Haussmann created wide boulevards, dividing up the city into the present 20 *arrondissements* (districts). A period of prosperity began in 1870. The Eiffel Tower was built for the World Exhibition in 1889, in 1900 the first Métro line opened and then followed the Belle Epoque: the days of Maxims, the Folies and the talents of Picasso, Hemingway, Monet and Renoir. The city has never looked back.

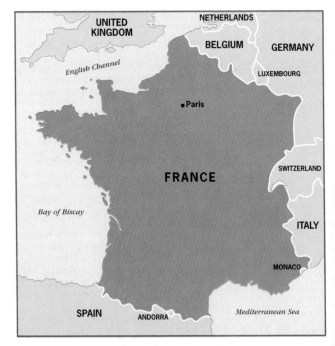

THE DIFFERENT AREAS

Paris is divided up into 20
different numbered areas or
arrondissements thanks to Baron
Haussmann, who sliced up the
city into neat sections to please
Napoleon III. The numbers start
at the centre of the city and work
outwards in a clockwise spiral.
As a general rule once you start
getting into double figures you
will need to use the Métro to get
around.

Each area has its own distinctive
character, from the sleazy red
light district in the 9e to the wide
boulevards and luxury hotels in
the neighbouring 8e (*er* or *e* is
the abbreviation used for
premier, deuxième, etc
arrondissement). Although the
boundaries are clearly defined
officially, some areas described
by name, like the Marais, spill
over into more than one
numbered area. Your first
decision is whether to stay on the
Right or the Left Bank of the River
Seine.

The **Right Bank** (**Rive Droite**) is,
on the whole, grander than

*The quais along the Seine are lined
with bouquinistes plying their
trade with second-hand books,
postcards and prints*

the Left. It is where the main
monuments are, the large
department stores, the *haute
couture* boutiques, the Louvre,
Beaubourg, the Tuileries, the
Opéra, the Champs-Elysées, the
Bastille and the Marais as well as
the red light area of Pigalle, and
gay (in the modern sense) Paris
around Les Halles.

The **Left Bank** (**Rive Gauche**) is
more Bohemian in parts but no
less chic. The Latin Quarter is
largely inhabited by students and
the ethnic population of the city,
but this side of the river also
includes the Eiffel Tower, the
Luxembourg Gardens, St-
Germain-des-Prés, the Musée
d'Orsay with its magnificent
collection of Impressionist
paintings, numerous boutiques,
art galleries, late night bars,
cafés, jazz clubs, street markets
and restaurants of every
nationality.

THE DIFFERENT AREAS

But Paris is small – all you have to do to get from one side to the other is nip over one of the bridges.

If you are unfamiliar with the city you may like to know a bit about the character of each *arrondissement* and the different areas. If you want a central hotel choose one in the following areas (in a rough rank order of preference): 6e, 1er, 8e, 2e, 4e, 5e, 7e, 3e, 9e, 10e, 14e, and forget about the rest unless you do not mind driving or taking public transport into the centre. For more about what to see within each area, see **What to See**, pages 21-44.

Right Bank (Rive Droite)

LOUVRE, PALAIS ROYAL (1er and 2e)

The centre of Paris, the Right Bank of the River Seine. Home of many of the large luxury hotels, the sort you arrive at by taxi rather than on foot. The area also includes the Louvre, the Conciergerie on the Ile de la Cité, the grand avenue leading up to the Opéra (which has airlines and tourist offices), an assortment of shops including fashionable boutiques and exclusive jewellers in and around the place Vendôme and to a lesser extent in the rue de Rivoli, the trendy boutiques in the place des Victoires, the antique shops opposite the Louvre, the Tuileries Gardens, many offices, and major institutions, the Bourse, the Bibliothèque National, and the arcaded 19th-century *passages* around the Palais Royal.

FORUM DES HALLES/BEAUBOURG (part of the 1er, 3e and 4e)

Touristy is the best way to

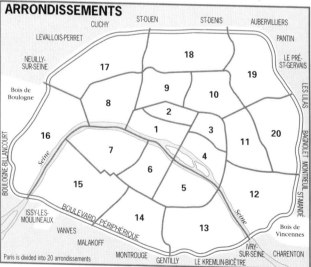

ARRONDISSEMENTS

Paris is divided into 20 arrondissements

describe this area. Still undecided as to its true identity, it is a mix of modern glass and chrome covering the largest underground shopping area in Europe, the Forum des Halles, and somewhat sleazy side streets around it with neons, cafés, and sex shops in the rue St-Denis and bars and jazz clubs towards Châtelet. Les Halles was Paris's main market, moving out after 800 years in 1969 and leaving a vast hole that was eventually filled by the shopping centre and neighbouring Beaubourg, the name given to the controversial inside-out Georges Pompidou Centre, containing the National Museum of Modern Art, opened in 1977 and now more popular than the Eiffel Tower. You can travel up the outside on an escalator from where there are splendid views of Notre-Dame, the Eiffel Tower and other major sites. The whole area is a mecca for visitors. The piazza in front of it is always packed with people watching the free street shows: jugglers, musicians, portrait painters and others entertaining the crowds. You can sit down and watch in one of the (expensive) cafés, if you can find a seat. It is not difficult to distinguish the Parisian offspring in their designer clothes from overseas children in grubby jeans and T-shirts. Central to stay in, but crowded.

The biggest free show in Paris takes place in the piazza outside Beaubourg

LES ILES (ST LOUIS, DE LA CITÉ) (4e, 1er)

Peaceful and relatively calm after the bustle of the main boulevards – though nevertheless pretty crowded, especially on warm afternoons. Two tiny islands in the Seine, where Paris began, right in the heart of the city and dominated by Notre-Dame Cathedral, the Palais de Justice, the Sainte-Chapelle and the Conciergerie. An area of shady squares and Seine views. The few hotels that are there are much sought after and difficult to get into.

The **Ile St Louis** is the quieter of the two islands with narrow streets – the main one running across the centre – and tall 17th-century houses. Named after a French king who came to meditate when it was just a cow pasture, it was settled in the early 17th century. You can relax on

THE DIFFERENT AREAS

the *quais* (there is a tree-lined walk) or have a drink or a snack in one of the bars or outdoor cafés.

The **Ile de la Cité** is approached by the Pont Neuf, the city's oldest bridge. This is where it all began, on a natural defence in the river, settled by the Romans. On the Ile de la Cité you will find the quiet place Dauphine, the Sainte-Chapelle with its splendid stained-glass windows and the Conciergerie where Marie Antoinette was imprisoned. There is a flower market in the place Louis-Lépine, with birds for sale on Sundays, and, of course, the magnificent Gothic Notre-Dame Cathedral. If you stand outside the cathedral's west door there is a spot on the pavement known as *kilomètre zéro* from which all distances in France are marked.

THE MARAIS, RÉPUBLIQUE (3e, 4e)

The Marais, on the Right Bank between Beaubourg and the Bastille, is one of the oldest and most interesting areas of Paris. It is relatively calm, quiet and devoid of traffic compared to other parts of Paris.

Once inhabited by the aristocracy, its fortunes changed with the Revolution when its proximity to the Bastille and its prison turned the elegant Marais into the all too familiar setting of Victor Hugo's *Les Misérables.* Although recently renovated it has been spared the bulldozers and most of the 17th-century mansions or *hôtels* as they are called have been carefully converted into offices, boutiques, apartments and

museums, including the magnificent Picasso Museum in the Hôtel Salé, the Hôtel Carnavalet in the rue de Sévigné (together with the neighbouring Hôtel le Peletier de St Fargeau housing the Museum of the History of the City of Paris), and the Museum Victor Hugo, in the great writer's house in the places des Vosges, Paris's most beautiful square with *hôtels*, interesting shops and several good restaurants beneath the arcades. Property prices have escalated and rooms once inhabited by the hungry poor are now filled with the hungry rich who are sitting on a potential gold mine, due to explode with the opening of the new Opera House for the 'people'. Designer boutiques, ultra modern furniture

Fountains play over revellers in place de la Concorde; in the distance the sedate façade of la Madeleine

showrooms and art galleries
open by the day, but the area is
still full of the old craftsmen. This
is where to come if you want a
picture framed or a handbag
repaired. It is also the centre of
the rag trade, and the home of
the Jewish community, with
synagogues and delis and
middle European restaurants
(some Russian) concentrated
between the rue des Ecouffes
and rue des Rosiers.

Paris's gay community
congregates in bars and discreet
clubs along the rue Ste-Croix-
de-la-Bretonnerie. But it is all
very low key and stylish. There
are also clubs and discos in the
quartier du Temple just south of
the République and just north of
the Hôtel-de-Ville.

The hotels in this area get
cheaper as you get towards the
République; some are in
converted mansions near the
place des Vosges.

CHAMPS-ELYSÉES, MADELEINE and PLACE DE LA CONCORDE (8e)

A big bustling area with
expensive hotels around the
Champs-Elysées, exclusive
fashion salons in the avenue
Montaigne and rue du Faubourg-
St-Honoré and fabulous food
shops (Fauchon, Hédiard) in the
place de la Madeleine, with high-
class tarts behind it in the rue de
Sèze.

The famous Champs-Elysées
stretches for 1.1 miles (1.8 km)
from the Arc de Triomphe to the
place de la Concorde, often one
long traffic jam, lined with neon-
lit cinemas, airline offices, banks,
bars, and overpriced restaurants
and cafés. You will also find the
Lido cabaret, and hordes of
weekend revellers who get off
the RER express train at Etoile
and hang around the Drugstore
and the fast-food outlets like
McDonalds and Burger King.

One of its famous landmarks,
Fouquets, where De Gaulle and
Churchill used to lunch, narrowly
escaped being turned into a
hamburger bar by its Kuwaiti
owners. The Government,
horrified at the prospect,
intervened and declared it a
national historic monument.

In the place de la Concorde you
will see the obelisk from the
Temple of Luxor in Egypt and the
grand de Crillon hotel, the only
luxury hotel left still owned by
the French.

This area does not have to be
prohibitively expensive. The
department stores are only just
over the boundary into the 9e,
the quieter residential area near
the Parc Monceau has medium
priced hotels and good

restaurants, and prices drop considerably towards the Gare St-Lazare which is still within walking distance of the centre.

OPÉRA, DEPARTMENT STORES and PIGALLE (9e)

The area with the largest number of hotels and probably the most mixed in character. It stretches from the busy boulevard Haussmann with the enormous department stores (Galeries Lafayette, Printemps, Monoprix and M&S), to the Paris Opéra, past major banks to the Folies Bergère and the sleazy low life of Clichy and Pigalle – the red light district with its strip clubs and sex shows.

You should avoid staying in the northern part of this *arrondissement* if you possibly can, even though numerous tour operators will try and persuade you otherwise. (See **Paris by Night**, pages 85–92.)

GARE DU NORD and GARE DE L'EST (10e)

Cheap, busy and generally a bit drab and depressing. This is where you will arrive if you come in by train from the airport. Your hotel may be noisy but it will cost a lot less than in other areas of Paris and if you are only looking for somewhere to put your head down, and do not intend to spend much time in it, you are not too far from the centre. Nothing much of interest to see.

BASTILLE (11e, 12e)

The Bastille, home of the famous prison stormed by angry mobs on 14 July 1789, is now *the* up-and-coming area of Paris. The new Opera House for the people

nearby, which looks much like an office block, was inaugurated on 13 July 1989.

The area is still mixed in character – alongside the modern art galleries, trendy nightclubs, brasseries, cafés and retro-fashion boutiques there are cheap furniture shops, a fairground and dingy bars. Nightlife concentrates itself in a triangle between the rue de Lappe, rue de Charonne and rue de la Roquette and includes an old music hall of the 1930s where old timers still dance Saturday afternoons away and the *branché* young queue up for rock bands in the evenings.

The neighbouring 12e is a suburb some way from the centre. It includes the Gare de Lyon and the vast Palais Omnisports de Bercy which offers large audiences anything from rock concerts to ice hockey matches.

The Seine is lined with old warehouses that are being slowly bought up by developers. Thousands of boats are moored on the western edge of the 12e in the Paris Arsenal. You can take a barge north up to La Villette (see pages 24–26), under the Bastille, or to explore the canals.

The 12e ends at the Périphérique on the edge of the Bois de Vincennes which has a zoo and a small boating lake (see **Parks and Gardens**, page 36).

THE 16e and 17e

The 16e, near the Bois de Boulogne, is where the most wealthy Parisians have their apartments. It is very chic, very fashionable and very expensive. There is little of interest for

Gleaming and efficient, high-speed trains dispatch visitors at the Gare du Nord

visitors apart from the shops in the boulevard Victor Hugo and avenue Foch, some of the best restaurants, the Palais de Chaillot, and the Palais de Tokyo (devoted to photography), and an impressive collection of Monet paintings in the Musée Marmottan. The village areas of Auteuil and Passy have more character, with fashionable boutiques in the rue de Passy. There are some elegant, old-fashioned hotels in the area if you do not mind being some way from the centre.

There are also comfortable hotels in the residential, though less exclusive, 17e and some huge modern luxury hotels catering for businessmen around the busy Porte Maillot and Palais des Congrès convention centre.

MONTMARTRE (18e)
The old artists' quarter topped by the icing sugar dome of

Sacré-Cœur Cathedral, sadly overrun by visitors having their portraits etched and sketched in the place du Tertre at the top of the hill. You can get a funicular up or walk on the quiet southwest side up the rue Lepic. Once at the top there are a number of (over-priced) open-air cafés, with accompanying accordionists and wonderful views across Paris from the Cathedral. To the south is the Marché Saint-Pierre, which sells colourful fabrics. There are ethnic shops in the surrounding streets. Property is cheap and there are plenty of reasonably priced hotels. The sleazy boulevard Clichy and boulevard Pigalle are at the bottom of the hill. To the north of Montmartre is the flea market at the Porte de Clignancourt.

THE DIFFERENT AREAS

The Brasserie Lipp, in the Latin Quarter on the Left Bank in St-Germain, is where to watch Parisians go by

THE 19e and 20e

The northeast of Paris. In the 19e is the site of the new Parc de Villette and its various attractions including the Cité des Sciences et de l'Industrie and the Buttes de Chaumont park. You may not want to stay so far out, as transport into the centre is time-consuming and expensive; there are few hotels. The 20e is even less inspiring. It includes the Père Lachaise cemetery and the weekend and Monday flea market for secondhand clothes at the Porte de Montreuil.

Left Bank (Rive Gauche)

THE LATIN QUARTER (5e, 6e)

For first-time visitors the Left Bank's Latin Quarter somehow feels more Parisian. It's livelier, the streets are narrower, the boutiques less formidable, the famous cafés in the boulevard St-Germain more crowded. The place St-Michel is the centre of the Latin Quarter proper, the 5e. The place St-Germain is the centre of the 6e, which is on the whole more expensive and more elegant than the student-land of the 5e.

The 5e includes the Panthéon, the Sorbonne university, the student and ethnic population of the city, the Jardin des Plantes, and one of the best food markets, in the rue Mouffetard. There are plenty of reasonably priced hotels and restaurants of every nationality, including numerous Greek and North African restaurants in the pedestrian-only rue de la Huchette, which also offers one of the few authentic jazz clubs, Le Caveau de la Huchette.

The new Institut du Monde Arabe in the quai Saint-Bernard, with its windows made up of giant lenses that open and shut with the sun, is also in the 5e. All in all, an area that appeals to those on a budget.

ST-GERMAIN (6e)

Centre of the arts and fashion world. Not *haute couture* but designer chic. A relatively small area on the other side of the Seine from the Louvre, centred around St-Germain-des-Prés and extending south to the Luxembourg gardens.

St-Germain-des-Prés gained its reputation after the war when its inexpensive restaurants and bars became the meeting place for intellectuals and artists. The cafés (Flore, Lipp and Deux Magots) frequented by Jean-Paul Sartre and Simone de Beauvoir are still there and everyone still watches the world go by, but the prices can be prohibitively expensive. There are numerous boutiques.

To the north of the boulevard St-Germain the narrow streets are full of small hotels, art galleries, bookshops, antique shops, elegant boutiques, and restaurants. The best streets for shopping are rue Jacob and the rue Bonaparte and, south of St-Germain, the place St-Sulpice and the Cherche-Midi. There is also a lively food market that takes up most of the rue de Buci and rue de Seine.

There are numerous hotels, some with pretty courtyards, many old 17th- and 18th-century houses with a steep climb up to the fifth-floor rooms. You will be a stone's throw from the Seine and the bridges across to the Right Bank. If you can find a hotel room in this area you should take it.

INVALIDES, MUSÉE D'ORSAY and THE EIFFEL TOWER (7e)

Quiet, staid and a bit lacking in atmosphere compared to other parts of Paris. But still very central. The buildings are magnificent 17th-, 18th- and 19th-century private residences, many of them ministries and embassies and the broad tree-lined streets are generally quiet unless you happen to be around

when one or other section of the population is demonstrating about something.

There are usually police in front of the high-walled private house of the Prime Minister and outside the Foreign Office.

To cater for the embassies and ministers, the 7e has a large number of Paris's best restaurants and some up-market designer boutiques in the rue de Grenelle and rue St-Dominique as well as the Au Bon Marché department store. The main sites are the Eiffel Tower, the new Musée d'Orsay in the old railway station, with its national art collection including Impressionist paintings, the Invalides, and the Rodin Museum.

Few visitors stay in this area of Paris, although there are numerous quiet hotels and it is easy to walk both to the Latin Quarter and across to the Louvre and Right Bank.

MONTPARNASSE (14e, 15e)

Both areas are huge, but provided you are staying in the north of either *arrondissement*, near to Montparnasse, you will not be too far from the centre. The steel and smoked-glass, 59-storey Tour Montparnasse was completed in the mid-1970s – somewhat of an eyesore, but there are splendid views of Paris from the top, and a large shopping complex at the foot of it. Like St-Germain-des-Prés, Montparnasse was a quarter associated with writers and artists, who used to hang out at the famous La Coupole restaurant and ballroom (newly renovated), as well as a working-class district. Today it is largely a commercial area with big hotels and office blocks. There are sex shops and clubs in the rue de la Gâité and plenty of cheap restaurants near the Cité Universitaire. Near by you will find the entrance to the catacombs on the place Denfert-Rochereau, and the Observatoire.

There are many relatively cheap modern hotels in the 15e which tour operators will try and tell you are near the centre. They are not.

THE 13e

No-man's land, the Gare d'Austerlitz, the Chinese quarter (with a market between the avenues de Choisy and d'Ivry) and the Gobelin tapestry factory which you can visit. Much of the area is taken over by tower-block flats where many of the immigrant population live, but there is still some Parisian character around the rue de la Butte-aux-Cailles with its little bars and bistros. The north of the area is near the 5e.

If you have the postal code of an address in Paris you can figure out the *arrondissement* that it is in. All Paris postal numbers are five digit numbers beginning with 750, the last two numbers are the *arrondissement*: thus 75015 would be in the 15e *arrondissement*, 75001 would be in the 1er.

La Coupole, a brasserie in Montparnasse, has always been popular with Parisian intellectuals, past and present

WHAT TO SEE

Museums

For years the ingredients of a Paris weekend were pretty standard: you went to the Louvre, perhaps to the Rodin Museum, to the Notre-Dame Cathedral, up the Eiffel Tower, took a stroll in the Luxembourg gardens and up the Champs-Elysées. If there was time you took a boat ride on the Seine, made a visit to Montmartre, strolled around the Latin Quarter and sat down for a bit to watch the world go by from one of the famous cafés.

While you can still do all that, there are some new attractions like the Musée d'Orsay national art gallery and the exciting Cité des Sciences at La Villette a suburb in the northeast of the capital.

The most popular sights in Paris (in rank order) are: the Pompidou Centre (Beaubourg),

Enter the Louvre through an eye-catching glass pyramid designed by Pei

the Eiffel Tower, the Louvre, the Cité des Sciences at La Villette, the Musée d'Orsay, La Géode at La Villette, the Arc de Triomphe and the Musée Picasso.

Under 18s, students and senior citizens get in free or at reduced rates in some museums; others offer free admission to everyone on Sunday. You buy a Carte Musées et Monuments giving unlimited access to museums for one, three or five days, from museums and tourist offices. The following galeries and museums are divided into **Essential Viewing** and **The Rest**. See also **The Different Areas** (pages 11–20), **Landmarks** (pages 30–35), **Parks, Gardens and Cemeteries** (pages 36–41) and **Excursions from Paris** (pages 41–44).

WHAT TO SEE – MUSEUMS

Essential Viewing

◆◆◆
**LOUVRE MUSEUM,
Palais du Louvre, 1er** ✓

quai du Louvre
Just east of the Tuileries Gardens on the Right Bank of the Seine, this former royal palace is now the largest museum in the world. The massive expansion programme continues until 1996. The innovative glass pyramid designed by the Chinese-American Pei, marks the entrance from Cour Napoléon to the six different departments: **Oriental Antiquities**, **Egyptian Antiquities**, **Greek and Roman Antiquities**, **Painting**, **Sculpture**, and **Furniture and Objets d'art**. Top of your list should be Leonardo da Vinci's *Mona Lisa*, the *Winged Victory of Samothrace* and *Venus de Milo*. There is no possibility of being able to 'do' it all at once, so pick out the works you particularly want to see, and do your best to find them.
An added attraction is the sumptuous Salon Impérial, one of the imperial apartments of the Palais Royal, rivalling Versailles for its opulence.
Open: 09.00 to 18.00 (Wednesday until 22.00 either the Denon or Sully wing).
Closed: Tuesday

◆◆◆
MUSÉE D'ORSAY, 7e ✓

Métro: Palais Royal, Louvre-Rivoli
1 rue de Bellechasse
Opened at the end of 1986, Impressionist paintings, fine and decorative arts, architecture and photography from 1848 to 1914 (variously moved from the Jeu de Paume, the Palais de Tokyo, and the Louvre) are now housed in the spectacularly renovated, airy Gare d'Orsay, the former railway station that served southwest France. A total of 2,300 paintings and 1,500 sculptures. The transformation took £13·5 million and 10 years.
Go straight to the top, third floor for Impressionist paintings: room upon room of the most famous works of Monet, Renoir, Cézanne, Pissarro, Sisley and Degas. The middle floor exhibits include sculpture by Rodin and Maillol, paintings by Bonnard and Vuillard, works representing Foreign Schools, Symbolism and Naturalism, and Art Nouveau furniture.
The ground floor has Decorative Arts 1850–1880 as well as Degas, Manet, Monet and Renoir pre-1870 and a good bookshop in the original buffet.
The Café des Hauteurs on the top floor has views through the old station clock over the Seine, and there is an outside terrace to get your breath back.
More formal meals are served in the sumptuous restaurant, with chandeliers, painted ceiling and statues. There are also changing exhibitions, concerts, films and lectures.
Open: 10.00 to 18.00 (to 21.45 Thursday); Sunday 09.00 to 18.00
Closed: Monday
Métro: Solférino, *RER:* Musée d'Orsay

In the Musée d'Orsay. Van Gogh's jollier pictures appeal to nearly everyone, no matter what their age

◆◆◆
**MUSÉE NATIONAL D'ART
MODERNE (National Museum
of Modern Art) – BEAUBOURG
or the GEORGES POMPIDOU
CENTRE), 4e**
*Rues Rambuteau, Saint-Martin
and Beaubourg*
The museum is on the third (1965
to present day) and fourth floor
(1905 to 1965) of the Beaubourg
centre with changing exhibitions
on the 5th floor.
A fascinating collection of
modern art from Bonnard to
Bacon and including works by
Rousseau, Picasso, Matisse,
Warhol and Balthus, right up to
the present day. There is much
going on in the rest of the
building (entry is free) which
includes a large cinema. There
are films on contemporary art,
activities for children, an
industrial design gallery, a music
research unit, and an excellent
international arts bookshop.
Open: 12.00 to 22.00 (weekends
10.00 to 22.00). Admission
charge for museum, but free
Sunday 10.00 to 14.00
Closed: Tuesday
Métro: Rambuteau, Hôtel -de-
Ville, *RER*: Châtelet-les-Halles

WHAT TO SEE – MUSEUMS

◆◆
MUSÉE PICASSO, Hôtel Salé, 3e

5 rue de Thorigny
Until a few years ago the Hôtel Salé, one of the most elegant mansions in the Marais, was in a dilapidated state and occupied by squatters. Today it houses the Picasso Museum and its exterior and splendid interior, including an elegant wrought-iron staircase (one of the finest in Paris), look much as they did in 1656 when Aubert de Fontenay, who made his fortune by levying *la gabelle*, a 'salt' tax (hence the name *salé)* lived there. In between times it was variously a home for rare books at the time of the Revolution, a school, the Venetian Embassy and the official residence of the Archbishop of Paris. As well as many of his lesser-known paintings from his 'blue' period to the 1920s, you can also see Picasso's own collection from his estate including works by Cézanne, Rousseau, Degas and Matisse.
Open: 09.15 to 17.15
(Wednesday to 22.00)
Closed: Tuesday
Métro: Chemin-Vert, Saint-Paul

LA VILLETTE, 19e
La Villette, in the northeast of Paris just inside the Périphérique (ring road), is a 136 acre (55ha) landscaped park created out of the old abattoirs and surrounded by two canal basins. It stretches from the Porte de la Villette to the Porte de Pantin. It takes about 15 minutes by Métro from central Paris to get there.
The new site includes a variety of venues, the most important of

which, if you have children with you, is:

◆◆◆
CITÉ DES SCIENCES ET DE L'INDUSTRIE, 19e ✓

30 avenue Corentin-Cariou
This vast museum encourages children and adults of all ages to learn about man, science and technology through games of discovery. There are several floors, all open-plan with escalators running up to each. It incorporates a Planetarium with an astronomical simulator and a sky of 10,000 stars, an 'Explora' on three levels which focuses on modern day discoveries, and Cité des Enfants (Children's City) where there are two discovery workshops for different age groups. The only problem is that the vast majority of instructions and the commentary at the Planetarium show (extra charge) are in French, although some of the computer games offer an English option and there are headphones to guide you through different areas. On the principle that children never read instructions anyway, however, it should not be beyond the majority of them to figure out how everything works. In the Cité des Enfants , they can, for example, bicycle alongside their own reflection to show how bones move, work a video telephone with a friend in a nearby booth, or film each other in a TV studio.
The Cité is split into four themes: Earth and the Universe, The Adventure of Life, Matter and Human Labour, Language and Communication. The

At the Picasso Museum – housed in a beautiful Marais mansion

surrounding *parc*, which has been ambitiously landscaped, includes the fighter submarine l'Argonaute, the Cinaxe simulator and a popular dragon slide for younger children.
Open: 10.00 to 18.00
Closed: Monday
Métro: see *How to Get There*, below

Also at La Villette:
Zénith, an enormous, inflatable pop and rock stadium across the canal that seats 6,500. You cannot miss it if you look for a red aeroplane.

La Grande Halle (the old cattle hall) is a huge structure of iron and glass. It has been converted for major concerts and exhibitions.

La Géode is a huge, mirrored silver globe surrounded by water, behind the Science

Museum. Inside there is a 180-degree hemispheric screen for lasers and cinerama-like films. The films are not particularly interesting (in French only) but you feel as if you are part of the setting, as the screen wraps itself around your lateral vision and your ears get used to six-track stereo.
Open: 10.00 to 21.00
Closed: Monday

How to Get There:
Métro: Porte de la Villette. Porte de Pantin Métro is nearer if you are going to Grande Halle only.
By barge: Canauxrama operate cruises along canal Saint Martin, leaving from the Port de l'Arsenal near the place de la Bastille (*Métro*: Bastille) or from the Bassin de la Villette, quai de la Loire (*Métro*: Jean-Jaurès.) The

*La Géode, the revolutionary
hemispheric cinema, at La Villette*

journey takes an hour and a
half. Or you can take the Paris
Canal barge (April to
November) from central Paris
just below the Musée d'Orsay
from the quai Anatole France, 7e.
You pass the Louvre and Notre-
Dame, travel under the place de
la Bastille, through locks and
under swing bridges to La
Villette.
The journey takes three hours
and there is an English
commentary.
Information and reservations
Canauxrama, the Bassin de la
Villette, 13 quai de la Loire, 19e
(tel: 42 39 14 00). Paris Canal,
19 quai de la Loire, 19e. (tel:
42 40 96 97).

The Rest

◆
**GRAND PALAIS, GALERIES
NATIONALES DU, 8e**
Avenue du Général Eisenhower
Built for the Paris Exhibition in
1900, a huge domed building with
large major exhibitions. Along the
entire façade of the Grand Palais
is a distinctive Iouic colonnade.
The **Petit Palais** across the
avenue Winston-Churchill has a
permanent collection of antiques
and paintings dating from
antiquity to the beginning of the
20th century (open 10.00 to
17.40, closed Monday).
Open: 10.00 to 20.00
(Wednesday to 22.00)
Closed: Tuesday
Métro: Champs-Elysées-
Clémenceau

◆
JEU DE PAUME, 1er
Tuileries Gardens
The Impressionist paintings have
moved to the Musée d'Orsay and
the gallery has been renovated
to house major exhibitions of
20th-century art.
Open: Tuesday 12.00 to 21.30;
Wednesday to Friday 12.00 to
19.00; Saturday and Sunday
10.00 to 19.00
Closed: Monday
Métro: Concorde, Tuileries

◆
MAISON DE VICTOR
HUGO, 4e
6 place des Vosges
Another insight into a Marais
mansion, the house in which
Victor Hugo (*Les Misérables*)
lived between 1832 and 1848. As
well as a writer, he was also a
painter and interior decorator
and 400 of his paintings as well
as replicas of rooms he
decorated are on show.
Open: 10.00 to 17.40
Closed: Monday
Métro: Saint-Paul, Bastille,
Chemin Vert

◆
MANUFACTURE NATIONALE
DES GOBELINS, 13e
42 avenue des Gobelins
Walk south from the Panthéon to
the Gobelin factory where you
can join a guided tour to see how
the famous tapestries are made.
Gobelin tapestries are
traditionally heavy wall hangings
depicting a range of subjects
from the seasons to royal
lifestyles and residences to
designs by French painters.
Open: guided tours on
Tuesday, Wednesday and

Thursday afternoons
Closed: rest of the week
Métro: Gobelins

◆◆
MUSÉE D'ART MODERNE DE
LA VILLE DE PARIS, 16e
11 avenue du Président-Wilson
Huge building with
contemporary works, works of
Cubism, the Paris School and
Matisse's *Danse* among them.
Also Art Deco furniture and
changing exhibitions.

*The courtyard linking the huge
Musée d'Art Moderne and the
Palais de Tokyo*

Open: 10.00 to 17.40
(Wednesday to 20.30)
Closed: Monday
Métro: Alma-Marceau, Iéna

◆
MUSÉE DES ARTS DE LA
MODE, 1er
109 rue de Rivoli
Fashion museum in the Pavillon
de Marsan in the Palais du

Louvre, in the Louvre complex. Four centuries of French fashion on the fifth floor with stunning displays of fabrics, accessories and costumes, many of them donated by famous names with life-sized mannequins made especially to fit the various outfits. Many temporary exhibitions and a large reference library.
Open: for temporary exhibitions only Wednesday to Saturday 10.00 to 18.00; Sunday 11.00 to 18.00
Closed: Monday and Tuesday
Métro: Palais Royal, Tuileries

◆◆
MUSÉE DES ARTS DÉCORATIFS, 1er
107 rue de Rivoli
On the ground floor. Interior design *à la française* from the Middle Ages to the present day. Private apartments, tapestries, glass, pottery, paintings and sculpture with a gallery of contemporary design that includes toys and crafts.
Open: Monday to Saturday 12.30 to 18.00; Sunday 11.00 to 18.00
Closed: Monday and Tuesday
Métro: Palais Royal, Tuileries

◆◆
MUSÉE CARNAVALET (MUSEE HISTORIQUE DE LA VILLE DE PARIS), 3e
23 rue de Sévigné
Within two neighbouring old *hôtels*, this museum portrays the history of the city from its origins to the present day, with emphasis on the French Revolution.
Open: 10.00 to 17.40
Closed: Monday
Métro: Saint-Paul, Chemin Vert

◆◆
MUSÉE DE CLUNY, Hôtel de Cluny, 5e
6 place Paul-Painlevé
On the Left Bank, at the crossroads of the boulevards St-Germain and St-Michel, a group of buildings, including one of three 15th-century houses left in Paris, Roman baths dating from AD 200 and the town residence of the Abbots of Cluny. The museum's galleries contain exhibits from the Middle Ages as well as furniture, sculptures, gold and silver up to the 15th century. It also has several well known 15th-century tapestries, the most perfect example of which is the series of six allegorical hangings, *The Lady and the Unicorn*.
Open: 09.30 to 17.15
Closed: Tuesday
Métro: Odéon, St-Michel

◆
MUSÉE DE L'INSTITUT DU MONDE ARABE, 5e
23 quai Saint-Bernard (entrance in rue des Fossés Saint-Bernard)
On the Left Bank. Worth visiting if you are interested in exhibits of the Arab world and for the architecture. The collection is housed in a modern building opened in 1987 with windows made up of lenses that open and shut with the sun (but do not do anything if it is dull). Good views from the 9th-floor terrace, where there is a restaurant.
Open: 10.00 to 18.00. Free
Closed: Monday
Métro: Jussieu, Sully-Morland

◆◆
MUSÉE MARMOTTAN, 16e
2 rue Louis-Boilly
After the Musée d'Orsay the next best gallery of Impressionist

Musée Rodin, where the sculptor lived until he died in 1917, has many of his most famous works in the house and garden

paintings. A private collection concentrating on Monet (also Renoir, Gauguin, Manet and Pissarro), alongside a remarkable collection of Empire-style furniture.
Open: 10.00 to 17.30
Closed: Monday
Métro: La Muette

◆◆
MUSEE DE L'ORANGERIE DES TUILERIES, 1er
Jardin des Tuileries
Impressionists up until the 1930s. Famous for the two oval rooms of Monet paintings that include the *Water Lilies*. Also Renoir, Matisse and Picasso.
Open: 09.45 to 17.15
Closed: Tuesday
Métro: Concorde, Tuileries

◆◆
MUSÉE RODIN, 7e
Hôtel Biron, 77 rue de Varenne
Between the Eiffel Tower and Musée d'Orsay, splendid museum in a rococo mansion devoted to Rodin's sculptures including *The Kiss* and *Adam and Eve* with others, including *The Thinker* in the garden.
Open: 10.00 to 17.00 (17.45 in summer)
Closed: Monday
Métro: Varenne, *RER*: Invalides

WHAT TO SEE

◆
PALAIS DE TOKYO, 16e
13 avenue du Président-Wilson
The Centre d'Exposition du
Patrimoine Photographique, in
the right wing has permanent
and temporary photography
exhibitions and a Cinémathèque.
Open: 09.45 to 17.00
Closed: Tuesday
Métro: Iéna

Churches and Monuments

◆◆◆
L'ARC DE TRIOMPHE DE
L'ÉTOILE, 8e ✓

Place Charles-de-Gaulle-Etoile
Twelve avenues, including the
Champs-Elysées, lead up to this,
one of Paris's most familiar
monuments, built by Napoleon
as a triumphal arch dedicated to

*The Arc de Triomphe sits squarely
at the top of the Champs Elysées,
dedicated to the military successes
of the armies of Napoleon*

the glory of the Imperial army.
The names of some 600 generals
are inscribed on the walls. The
tomb of the unknown soldier
reminds the world of the soldiers
who died for their country. You
can climb to the top for views but
they are not as good as those
from Beaubourg or the Eiffel
Tower. Access is via a subway
from the north pavement of the
Champs-Elyées.
Open: 10.00 to 17.00, (17.45 in
summer)
Closed: Public holidays
Métro: Charles-de-Gaulle-Étoile

◆◆
CONCIERGERIE, 4e
1 quai de l'Horloge,
Ile de la Cité
French history laid bare in a
14th-century Gothic setting. This
was where Marie Antoinette
awaited her fate (you can see her
cell, as well as much evidence of
the Revolution, the prisons and
the kitchens). Combine with a
visit to Notre-Dame, Sainte-

Chapelle and the Palais de Justice.
Open: 09.30 to 18.00
Métro: Cité, Châtelet

♦
ÉCOLE MILITAIRE, 7e
Avenue de la Motte-Picquet
A splendid 18th-century building near the Eiffel Tower and les Invalides, the Military Academy, used by the army as an officers' training college. You cannot go in.
Métro: École-Militaire

♦♦♦
EIFFEL TOWER (TOUR EIFFEL), 7e ✓

Champs de Mars
Built as a monument to the Great Exhibition of 1889 1,007 feet (307m) high. One of the most famous landmarks but these days less popular with visitors than Beaubourg. You can take a lift to the viewing platforms (1st, 2nd and 3rd) or if you are fit climb the steps (cheaper) as far as the second level, then take the lift to the top from where the views, on a clear day, extend for some 45 miles (72km).
There is an audio-visual of the history of the tower on the first stage, and bars and restaurants including the highly regarded Jules Verne restaurant on the second floor of the south leg, with its own private lift – one of the very best restaurants in Paris.
Open: 10.00 to 23.00 (24.00 Friday, Saturday and public holidays, April to early September, and daily in July and August)
Métro: Trocadéro, Bir-Hakeim

♦♦♦
LES INVALIDES, (MUSÉE DE L'ARMÉE), 7e ✓

Place Vauban
The Hôtel National des Invalides was built as a home for wounded soldiers by Louis XIV; it houses the Musée de l'Armée which has a collection of weapons and uniforms. There are also two churches here: St Louis des Invalides contains the tombs of soldiers, and the Eglise du Dôme, surmounted by its famous dome, holds the tomb of Napoleon.
Open: 10.00 to 17.00 (18.00 in summer)
Métro: Latour-Maubourg, Invalides

♦♦
MADELEINE, 8e
Place de la Madeleine
An unusual looking church dedicated to St Mary Magdalen, built to look like a Greek temple complete with Corinthian columns. Catholic services are held there.
Métro: Madeleine

♦♦♦
NOTRE-DAME CATHEDRALE, 4e
Ile de la Cité
One of the world's architectural masterpieces, a place of worship since pagan times, completed in the 14th century. An awe-inspiring exterior of Gothic extravagance, with gargoyles, gabled carved doorways and magnificent rose windows. Inside a vast echoing hall, 115 feet (35m) high, that can hold 9,000 worshippers at any one time. The pillars are Gothic, the aisles are flanked by chapels and flying

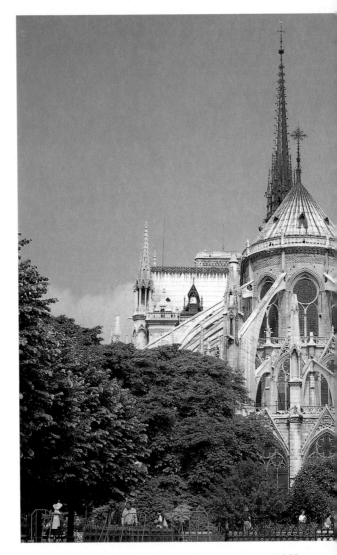

buttresses support the roof. If you want to know what is what, tag along behind one of the numerous English-speaking guides or join a tour (10.00 to 17.00 winter; 10.00 to 12.00 and 14.00 to18.00 summer). You can climb to the top of the towers,

Notre-Dame Cathedral on the Ile de la Cité, a Gothic masterpiece begun in 1163. There are fine views from the 226-foot (69m) tower

stroll in the public garden and visit the museum in the crypt to see the remains of the original cathedral. Outside the west door, on the pavement, *kilomètre zéro* marks the spot from which all distances in France are measured.
Open: 08.00 to 19.00 (towers 10.00 to 16.30; 17.30 summer)
Métro: Cité, *RER*: Saint Michel

◆◆
OPÉRA DE PARIS-GARNIER, 9e
Place de l'Opéra
Near the large department stores. Pop in to admire Chagall's wonderful ceiling, the grand staircase and spectacular marble foyer. That is if you have not got tickets for the ballet which is performed here; the opera is now at Opéra-Bastille.
Open: 11.00 to 17.00
Closed: August
Métro: Opéra

◆
PALAIS DE CHAILLOT, 16e
Place du Trocadéro
Now a theatre (with shows for children), cinema and several galleries and museums including the Musée National des Monuments Français. There are views from the terrace of the gardens, fountains and across towards the Seine and the Eiffel Tower.
Open: (museum) 09.00 to 18.00
Closed: Tuesday
Métro: Trocadéro

◆
PALAIS DE JUSTICE, 4e
Boulevard du Palais
The Law Courts are on the Ile de la Cité, an extravagant series of Gothic buildings separated by courtyards and incorporating

Sacré Cœur – built by the Catholics of France as a symbol of contrition and hope

Sainte-Chapelle. Tours are available. Combine with Notre-Dame Cathedral.
Open: weekdays 09.00 to 17.00
Métro: Cité, *RER*: Saint Michel

◆
PANTHÉON, 5e
Place du Panthéon
Impressive-looking former church on the highest point on the Left Bank, with a rather disappointing interior housing the 18th- and 19th-century tombs of, among others, Voltaire, Victor Hugo, Rousseau, Emile Zola and Jean Moulin. You can visit the

crypt.
Open: 10.00 to 12.30 and 14.00 to 17.30 (18.00 in summer)
Métro: Cardinal Lemoine

◆◆
SACRÉ-COEUR, 18e
Parvis du Sacré Cœur
Cupolas topped by an icing-sugar dome, famous on Paris's skyline (you can see it from the escalator outside the Georges Pompidou Centre). Built at the end of the 19th century, at the top of Montmartre with views of around 30 miles (48km) from the dome. The campanile is 262 feet (80m) high. Catholic visitors from the world over come to light their candles. Steep climb up or funicular from the Marché Saint-

Pierre.
Open: 06.00 to 23.00
Métro: Anvers, Abesses

◆◆◆
SAINTE-CHAPELLE, 1er
Boulevard du Palais
Splendid Gothic architecture
with the oldest stained-glass
windows in Paris, illustrating the
old and new testaments, dating
from the 13th century. Combine
with Notre-Dame, the
Conciergerie and the Palais de
Justice.
Open: 09.30 to 16.30 (18.00 in
summer)
Métro: Cité, *RER*: Saint Michel

◆
TOUR MONTPARNASSE, 15e
33 avenue du Maine
On the Left Bank. When it was
built it was the tallest office
building in Europe at 679 feet
(207m) high. Somewhat of an
eyesore, it has a restaurant, bar
and an observatory on the 56th
floor and a further open-air
viewing area on the 59th floor
with 360-degree views. On a
clear day you can see for some
25 miles (40km). Free lift if you
go up to the restaurant.
Open: 10.00 to 22.00 (23.00
Friday, Saturday and public
holidays and daily from April to
September)
Métro: Montparnasse-Bienvenüe

Squares

◆
PLACE DAUPHINE, 1er
Gravel-filled 17th-century
peaceful square with trees, on
the Ile de la Cité. You can have
tea at Fanny's.
Métro: Pont Neuf

◆◆◆
PLACE DE LA CONCORDE, 8e
The largest and craziest square
in Paris with one of Paris's top
hotels, the de Crillon, in pole
position. The traffic is frightening.
The famous 75-foot (23m) high
obelisk comes from the Temple
of Luxor and is covered in
hieroglyphics. It is floodlit at
night and there are great views
up the Champs-Elysées to the
Arc de Triomphe. Near the
Tuileries Gardens and the
Louvre.
Métro: Concorde

◆
PLACE DES VICTOIRES, 2e
Louis XIV architecture and
designer boutiques under
awnings. No fuss, no frills, just
trendy. You may see the
designer Kenzo.
Métro: Bourse

◆◆
PLACE DES VOSGES, 4e
In the heart of the restored
Marais, the oldest square in Paris
and some say the most beautiful,
built by Henry IV for festivals and
ceremonies and surrounded by
elegant mansions or *hôtels*.
Open-air restaurants and antique
shops under the arcades. Newly
landscaped gardens.
Métro: Chemin Vert

◆◆
PLACE VENDÔME, 1er
Built under Louis XIV, an
impressive 17th-century square
of great architectural merit with
Napoleon on a column
overseeing the *haute couture*
boutiques and expensive
jewellers. In between the Opéra
and the Tuileries gardens.
Métro: Tuileries

WHAT TO SEE

Parks and Gardens

◆
BOIS DE BOULOGNE, 16e
On the western edge of Paris running alongside the fashionable 16e. Popular haunt, by night, of prostitutes but safe enough by day. The 2,088 acres (845ha) include the famous Longchamp and Auteuil racecourses. There are numerous lakes and ponds for boating, mini-golf and bowling, and bikes for hire. A folk museum, Shakespeare theatre, restaurants, children's playgrounds, outdoor pool and camping possibilities, though heavily booked in summer.
Métro: Porte Dauphine, Porte Maillot, Porte d'Auteuil

◆
BOIS DE VINCENNES, 12e
On the southeast side of Paris in 2,459 acres (995ha). Including the Vincennes racecourse, Paris's best zoo, a museum of African and Oceanic art, Buddhist temple, working farm, château, three boating lakes, restaurants and Punch and Judy for children. You can also hire bikes.
Métro: St-Mandé-Tourelle, Porte-Dorée.

◆
JARDIN D'ACCLIMATATION, 16e
On the northern edge of the Bois de Boulogne in 25 acres (10ha). *The* park for children, with special attractions during the school holidays, at weekends and on Wednesdays in term-time. Range of things to go on (all costed individually), camel and pony rides, toy trains. Cafés and restaurants.
Métro: Les Sablons, Porte Maillot

◆◆
JARDIN DES PLANTES, 5e
Botanical garden with more than 10,000 classified plants, maze and small zoo in 70 acres (28 hectares). Also winter garden with rare flora from the Alps, the Pyrénées and the North Pole. There are several natural history museums, including Muséum National d'Histoire Naturelle (57 rue Cuvier), with fossils, minerals, anatomy and palaeontology, plus changing art exhibitions.
Open: (museum) 10.00 to 17.00
Closed: Tuesdays. Entrance fee.
Métro: Gare d'Austerlitz, Jussieu

◆
JARDIN DES SERRES D'AUTEUIL, 16e
Rare arboretum. Ninety-four hothouses with rare tropical plants, 140 varieties of camellia, orchids, palmarium.
Open: 10.00 to 17.00 (18.00 March to September)
Métro: Porte d'Auteuil

◆◆
JARDIN DU LUXEMBOURG, 6e
Choose this or the Tuileries for your Sunday afternoon stroll. Sixty-two acres (26ha) against a backdrop of the Palais du Luxembourg built for Marie de Medici, Henry IV's widow, to remind her of the Palazzo Pitti and Boboli Gardens in Florence. Watch little Parisians sail their boats on the pond, old men play *boules* and arm-linked lovers stroll the tree-lined avenues. Keep off the grass.
RER: Luxembourg

Parc de Bagatelle, known for its roses, irises and water lilies

◆◆◆
JARDIN DES TUILERIES, 1er
Opposite the place de la Concorde. Sixty acres (24ha) designed by Le Nôtre stretching from the place de la Concorde to the place du Carrousel, including a splendid Orangerie, with the Musée de Orangerie des Tuileries, and the Jeu de Paume, now renovated to house major temporary exhibitions of 20th-century art. A mini Arc de Triomphe built in 1805 commemorates Napoleon's victories, smaller than the real one which you can see by taking the path through the centre of the gardens.
Métro: Tuileries, Concorde

◆◆
JARDIN DU MUSÉE RODIN, 7e
77 rue de Varenne
Well worth a visit for its 2,000 rose bushes and copies of world-famous sculptures by Rodin, as well as the house.
Open: Wednesday to Sunday 10.00 to 17.00 (17.45 in summer)
Closed: Monday and Tuesday
Métro: Varenne, *RER*: Invalides

◆
PARC DE BAGATELLE, 16e
Sixty acres (24ha) of the Bois de Boulogne with rose gardens (international exhibition 1 to 30 June), tulip exhibitions (mid-March to mid-April), hundreds of water lilies, a pond and a restaurant.
Open: 09.00 to 18.00
Métro: Pont de Neuilly

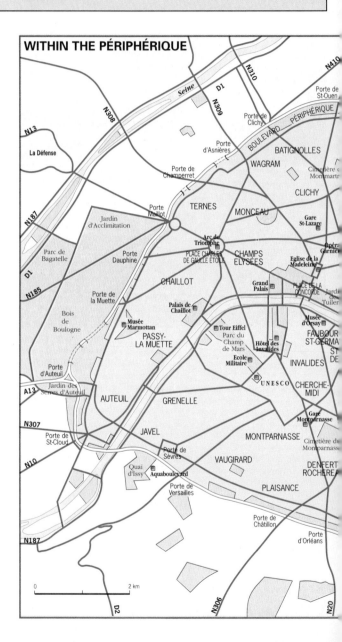

WITHIN THE PÉRIPHÉRIQUE

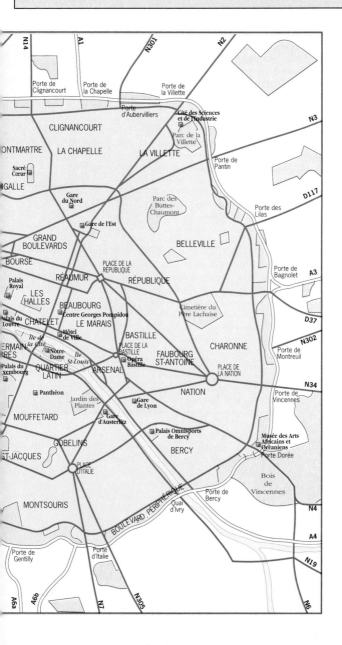

WHAT TO SEE

◆
PARC DES
BUTTES-CHAUMONT, 19e
In the north of Paris, 67 acres
(27ha) including a lake and
waterfall, bandstand, children's
playground, two restaurants and
a café. There are splendid views
from the little temple in the lake
across to Sacré-Cœur in
Montmartre.
Métro: Buttes-Chaumont, Botzaris

◆
PARC MONCEAU, 17e
Boulevard de Courcelles
Twenty three acres (9ha) of 18th-
century gardens with pagodas.
Pleasantly wooded nanny
territory with children's
playground and sandpit. Also
roller-skating rink.
Métro: Monceau

Cemeteries
You may wonder why on earth
you would want to include a visit
to a cemetery on your Paris
itinerary, but the graves and
tombstones of artists, writers and
celebrities, and not just French
ones, are fascinating, the
sculptures on the tombs are
works of art, and the grounds
themselves are a peaceful
retreat from the bustle of city life.

◆
CIMETIERE DE MONTMARTRE,
18e
20 avenue Rachel
The last resting place of Dumas,
the composers Offenbach and
Berlioz, Emile Zola (though his
remains are in the Panthéon) and
Degas. You can wander through
part of it if you are walking up to
Sacré-Cœur.
Métro: Blanche

◆
CIMETIERE DU
MONTPARNASSE, 14e
3 boulevard Edgar Quinet
Laid out in 1824. Tombs of Sartre,
Baudelaire, and Guy de
Maupassant.
Métro: Edgar Quinet

◆◆
CIMETIERE DU PERE-LACHAISE,
20e
Boulevard de Ménilmontant
Père-Lachaise is Paris's largest
cemetery with some stunning
sculptures and beautiful tombs

Parc Monceau was designed to look like a late 18th-century English and German garden

packed fairly closely together in tree-lined avenues, including a moving Monument for the Dead, built in 1900. Among the cast list of celebrities buried there are: Molière, Balzac, Bellini, Chopin, Bizet, Oscar Wilde, Proust, the actress Sarah Bernhardt, Edith Piaf and Jim Morrison the American rock star. Ask the custodian for a plan of the grounds. *Métro*: Père Lachaise

Excursions from Paris

There are many worthwhile places to visit from Paris. Most can be reached by public transport. You can also join coach tours, with a guide, if you do not mind having to keep up with the pace or paying more than the cost of travelling independently.

◆◆◆
CHARTRES

Wonderful cathedral city, with the huge Gothic 13th-century Cathedral of Notre-Dame itself (the nave is the widest in France and the crypt the largest) the main reason for a visit. Eighty-eight miles (142km) from Paris. Five-and-a-half hour coach tours include a guided tour of the cathedral. Or train from Gare de Montparnasse (every hour).

EURO DISNEY
See page 98

◆◆◆
FONTAINEBLEAU
(CHATEAU DE)

Renaissance palace in the middle of a forest with French and Italian interior: Gobelins tapestries, frescoes and paintings. You can visit the apartments where Louis XIII was born and the *petits appartements* of Napoleon and Josephine. In Josephine's bedroom there are silk wall hangings and matching chairs and curtains that took a workshop in Lyon 20 years to reproduce. The recently opened **Musée Napoléon** in the Louis XV wing of the building has a collection donated to the State by the Royal Family with paintings, china and furniture.

Reached by SNCF train from

WHAT TO SEE

Gare de Lyon (50 mins).
Open: 09.30 to 12.30 and 14.00
to 17.00
Closed: Tuesday
See also pages 48–51 for the
Forest of Fontainebleau.

◆◆
GIVERNY
Small village in southeast
Normandy, Claude Monet's
home. You can see the
landscape that inspired one of
France's greatest Impressionist
painters, his home, studio and
gardens, with the magnificent lily
pond and famous Japanese
bridge. Five-hour coach tours
are available. Or take the SNCF
train from St-Lazare to Vernon 50
minutes) and then bus to
Giverny.

*The Renaissance château of
Fontainebleau, with its splendid
English garden and parterre*

(*Open*: April to October.
Gardens 10.00 to 18.00, house
from 10.00 to 12.00 and 14.00 to
18.00
Closed: Monday

◆◆
MALMAISON
Napoleon's château bought for
Josephine. Tours, in French only,
take about an hour and a quarter;
it is tiny compared to Versailles
or Fontainebleau (it is best to see
those first).
The museum contains the
Bonapartes' possessions as well
as items from the Tuileries, St-
Cloud and Fontainebleau.

Josephine's apartments include her jewellery and perfumes and bills for her dresses. After her death it was discovered that she owed three million francs. Lovely gardens and a park to walk around. Five and a half miles (9km) from Porte Maillot. Three-and-a-half hour coach tours are available. Or take the RER from Charles-de-Gaulle-Étoile to La Défense (5 mins), then the 158A bus (25 mins), then walk (10 mins).
Open: 10.00 to 12.00 and 13.30 to 17.00
Closed: Tuesday

◆◆
SAINT-CLOUD
Park in a residential suburb on the south bank of the Seine, designed by Le Nôtre as part of a royal residence. Near the Pasteur Institute. Good views of Paris from the Rond Point de la Balustrade, fountains, terraces and Trocadéro garden and **Musée Historique** (Wednesday, Saturday and Sunday 14.00 to 18.00; 17.00 in winter). Two miles (3km) from Porte de St-Cloud, west of Paris.
Métro: Pont de Sèvres – Pont de St-Cloud (last stop, line 10)

◆◆◆
SAINT-DENIS
Visited mainly for its 12th-century Gothic **cathedral** (the model for Chartres), burial place of many kings and queens of France, as well as Saint Denis, a 3rd-century evangelist who kept on walking after he had been decapitated in Montmartre. You can see archaeological exhibits and medieval ceramics in the **Musée d'Art et d'Histoire**, rue Gabriel-Peri (open 10.00 to

17.30, Sunday 14.00 to 18.00; closed Tuesday). Six miles (9 km) from Porte de la Chapelle on the motorway. Or Métro to Saint-Denis-Basilique (line 13 from St-Lazare).
Cathedral open: 10.00 to 17.00 (19.00 in summer)

◆◆
SAINT GERMAIN-EN-LAYE
If you have time to spare, worth visiting for the Renaissance château which houses the **Musée des Antiquités Nationales**. The attractive grounds have a Grande Terrasse designed by Le Nôtre.
Picnic in nearby woods, and visit the priory. Nine miles (14km) from Porte Maillot. RER Line A to Saint-Germain-en-Laye.
Museum open: 09.30 to 17.30
Closed: Tuesdays

◆◆
SÈVRES
For lovers of pottery and ceramics. The famous multi-coloured **Musée National de la Céramique** contains samples as well as porcelain from around the world. Two miles (3km) from Porte de St Cloud.
Open: 10.00 to 17.15
Closed: Tuesday

◆◆
LES TRIANONS
See **Versailles** below

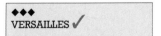
VERSAILLES ✓

If you have to choose one place to visit outside Paris, make it this one. Allow plenty of time. Unfortunately it is always crowded, especially on Sundays when the entrance fee is

WHAT TO SEE

reduced. Originally a hunting lodge, Louis XIII's sumptuous château, built in 1631, was made even grander by Louis XIV (to house 3,000 courtiers) with the help of Le Brun, Le Vau and Le Nôtre who landscaped the gardens. Most people do not have time to see everything. There are guided tours available. Priorities should be: the 246-foot (75m) long Hall of Mirrors, the most famous room in the palace, although the glass is not original; the State Apartments; the white and gold Chapel (all of which you can see without a guide) and the gardens (which are free).

If you visit on a summer Sunday the fountains may be on (check with the tourist office for specific dates and times) otherwise the statues look a bit sad. You can stroll along the formal terraces and parterres, see the Orangery and numerous statues, and find relative peace as you wander further away from the palace. There are always renovations going on at Versailles (which might close one or more

Versailles, home of 17th and 18th-century French kings, and model for other royal residences

galleries). The renovated apartments of the Dauphin and Dauphiness and of Louis XV's daughters are now open.

◆◆
LES TRIANONS are lesser palaces. The **Grand Trianon** is lavish with a pink marbled façade, the **Petit Trianon** less so. You get there by walking from the Neptune Gate along the avenue de Trianon.

Versailles is 8 miles (13km) from Porte d'Auteuil.
Three-and-a-half hour, and longer, escorted coach tours are available. RER Line C from Les Invalides to Versailles Rive Gauche (takes half an hour).
Open: 09.45 to 17.00
Closed: Monday
Reduced prices on Sundays but hardly worth it as you may have to queue.

PEACE AND QUIET

Wildlife and Countryside in and around Paris
by Paul Sterry

France's capital city lies on a low-lying basin known as the Ile de France which is dominated by the meandering Seine. In the hills surrounding the basin, the French aristocracy built splendid châteaux surrounded by parks and formal gardens. At the time they were built, each was sited in its own tract of woodland, maintained for private hunting. Despite recent urban sprawl, most of the château woodlands have remained more or less intact to this day. Were it not for the private and in some cases formerly royal status of the forests, the Paris basin would undoubtedly have lost much more of its woodland to development than it has.

Not surprisingly, most of the wildlife interest of the Ile de France is also associated with woodland, which would after all have been the dominant vegetation before man's influence was fully felt. Woods as close as 12 miles (20km) to Paris have plenty to offer, but to see lowland forest at its best you must travel south to Fontainebleau (see pages 41, 48–49). This forest is not only good by the standards of the Paris basin but is also one of the finest in the whole of France.

Parks and Formal Gardens

In terms of wildlife interest, the centre of Paris is much like any other European city. The inevitable feral pigeons and house sparrows congregate wherever there is a meal to be had and, in the winter, starlings roost on some of the buildings. Within the city itself, the Bois de Boulogne is, in spring and summer, a leafy park modelled on London's Hyde Park. Although scenically attractive, there is little natural vegetation within its boundaries because it was replanted with acacias and sycamores after Napoleon's troops wrecked the native oak woodland in 1815. You should also be warned that it has a reputation for being unsafe after dark so enjoy it during the daylight hours.

Almost all the châteaux surrounding Paris have formal gardens, many of which are open to the public and some, such as Ermenonville, have English-style parkland as well. The most famous of all Paris's formal gardens are those surrounding the Palais de Versailles, 15 miles (25km) south of Paris on the A13. However, the gardens at Chantilly, famous for its pastries and lace, although on a more modest scale are equally attractive.

The Bois de Boulogne lies on the western edge of Paris, alongside the Périphérique. Tracks, paths, woodland and lakes provide wildlife and scenic interest and, within its boundaries, the Parc de Bagatelle is renowned for its rose gardens and floral displays. The 2,459-acre (995ha) Bois de Vincennes, on the southeast of Paris, harbours the zoo, the Vincennes racecourse and formal gardens. Woodland and parkland birds can be found here, especially in spring and summer.

Checklist of common birds of parks and gardens

mallard	R
black-headed gull	R
woodpigeon	R
swallow	S
white wagtail	R
dunnock	R
robin	R
blackbird	R
song thrush	R
blue tit	R
great tit	R
chaffinch	R
house sparrow	R

R   year-round resident
S   summer visitor

Rivers and Lakes

Most of the rivers, lakes and ponds in and around the centre of Paris are either man-made or have been changed significantly from their natural state. Lakes like the one in the Bois de Boulogne are too ornamental and disturbed to hold anything more than feral ducks and geese, swans and black-headed gulls. In the forests and farmland surrounding the city, however, there are plenty of natural and semi-natural water bodies, supporting water-loving plants and animals, each acting like a magnet to the wildlife of the surrounding land. The Forest of Chantilly contains natural lakes known as les Etangs de Comelle, and there are numerous woodland pools and lakes in the Forests of Ermenonville and Rambouillet. The richest and most extensive areas of wetland in the region are found within the Forest of Fontainebleau.

Checklist of wildlife interest on freshwater

kingfisher	R
grey heron	R
sand martin	S
swallow	S
pochard	W
tufted duck	W
moorhen	R
coot	R
black tern	S
reed warbler	S
dragonflies	S
mayflies	S
yellow iris	S
water lily	S

R   year-round resident
S   summer only
W   most frequently seen in winter

Lake in the Bois de Boulogne

The Kingfisher

Kingfishers are without doubt the most colourful birds that visitors are likely to see around Paris: the plumage comprises a mixture of orange-red and several shades of blue. They are invariably found near water and often perch on overhanging branches. Kingfishers are master fishermen, diving into the water to catch small fish. These are dispatched by a swift blow against the perch and either swallowed whole or fed to their young during the breeding season. Kingfishers nest in burrows excavated into banks. At the end of the breeding season, the burrow is a smelly mess of droppings and fish bones.

Château Forests

The châteaux, which ring the outskirts of Paris at a discreet distance, were once the homes of the French nobility. They catered for their every need and so, in addition to the grand houses and formal gardens, most of them had private forests devoted to the nobility's main outdoor pursuit – hunting. Nowadays, many of these woodlands are open to the public, or at least can be viewed when visiting the château. Despite their proximity to Paris, they hold a wide variety of interesting wildlife.

The forest of Marly, on either side of the A13 autoroute to Normandy, has glades through oak, beech and sweet chestnut woodland, and roe deer are sometimes seen on the forest rides. There are also pleasant woodland walks through the Forest of St-Germain, 15 miles (25km) northwest of Paris on the N13. Situated near St-Germain-en-Laye, the birthplace of Debussy, the elevation of the forest affords excellent views of the meandering Seine.

Red squirrels can be seen throughout France. Although pinewoods are the preferred habitat of these agile climbers, the less disturbed beechwoods of the Paris basin harbour these charming animals.

Although not as rich as the Forest of Fontainebleau (see pages 48–49, 50–51), the woods around Versailles, Chantilly and Rambouillet still hold some of the

region's special birds, notably middle-spotted woodpecker and short-toed treecreeper.
Versailles lies 15 miles (25km) south of Paris on the A13, Rambouillet is southwest of Paris on the D906 and Chantilly is north of Paris on the N16.
Insect life is most abundant in the summer. The air is sometimes filled with the audible buzzing of flies and bees and several species of bush-cricket chirp from the foliage along tracks and paths.
Woodland rides are also the haunt of butterflies as they seek out flowers or shafts of sunlight. Speckled woods occur from May to September and are true sun-worshippers, spending hours on end basking in the heat. They are extremely territorial insects and will vigorously fight off intruders of the same species.

In spring, beechwoods around Paris are full of bird song

Speckled woods are grey-brown in colour with paler speckled markings on both the upper and lower wings. Their caterpillars feed on various grasses.

Fontainebleau
Of all the woodlands of the Paris basin, Fontainebleau is by far the most outstanding. With over 1,200 species of flowering plant recorded within its boundaries, 20 of which are orchids, it is one of the finest lowland forests in the whole of France. Fontainebleau has the advantage over many woodlands in other parts of France of having open public access. Although driving is restricted to the lanes and roads, you can walk anywhere along the leafy tracks and paths, some of which are signposted routes, and discover secret glades and clearings. It is also easily reached from Paris, being less than 44 miles (70km) to the south along the N7 and with frequent train services from the centre.
The charming village of Barbizon is perhaps one of the most attractive starting points from which to explore the area. Although most parts of the 61,775-acre (25,000ha) Forest of Fontainebleau are rewarding and marked trails and paths abound, the Gorges de Franchard is an outstanding area.
The French Institut Géographique National produce a map to the *Forêt de Fontainebleau*, (number 401). The scale of 1:25,000 should enable you to find your bearings and not get lost.
The secret of Fontainebleau's richness lies in its variety of habitats, this in turn a result of the different types of soil and

The crested tit is a year-round woodland resident

bedrock found in the region. Extensive beech woods favour the lime-rich areas while oak and birch are dominant on acid soils. Patches of heathland can be found on dry sandy soils, and in wetter areas the heath merges into bog. Where the soil is less acid, fenland and marshland vegetation predominate. To complete the variety, there are dramatic outcrops and gorges of both sandstone and limestone, some large enough to provide weekend practise sites for climbing enthusiasts. Fontainebleau is big enough and varied enough to have wild boar roaming its more secluded areas. You would be lucky to see *them*, but the deer which are also here should be easier to spot! As might be expected in such an exciting area, the birdlife is very rich, a roll-call of species that would do credit to northern and eastern Europe.

Woodland Birds

The further away from Paris you travel, the richer the woodland birdlife becomes and particularly in the forests around Fontainebleau.

In the spring, undisturbed patches of woodland come alive with birdsong. Nightingales and blackcaps are common in suitable habitat and compete with a variety of other warblers. The beautiful descending trill of the willow warbler is heard from open patches of birch and willow whilst wood warblers frequent stands of ancient beech. The song of the latter is a distinctive trill which speeds up as it goes along, and has been likened to a small coin spinning on a metal plate!

If you are very fortunate, you may hear France's most colourful woodland bird, the golden oriole, colourful both in terms of song and appearance.

The song consists of a series of loud flute-like whistles, reminiscent of something from a tropical forest. Although the bird itself is bright yellow, it remains hidden in the tree canopy and is seldom seen.

Fontainebleau's Woodpeckers

The Forest of Fontainebleau is one of the few places in Europe where you stand a reasonable chance of seeing six species of woodpecker in a single visit. Its fame has spread far and wide and birdwatchers are known to make the pilgrimage to Fontainebleau specifically to search for woodpeckers.

The best time of year to search for woodpeckers is in late winter, before there are any leaves on the trees to obscure your view, and when the birds begin calling at the start of the breeding season. Since they all have distinctive, and often loud, calls and 'drum' with their beaks on tree trunks, they are easily located by tracking the source of the sound.

Three of the woodpecker species have black, white and red plumages in varying amounts. The sparrow-sized lesser-spotted woodpecker has neat black and white barring on its back, distinct from the two larger species which have a conspicuous white patch on each wing. To separate these two you must look carefully at their heads. Middle-spotted woodpeckers always have a bright red cap and white cheeks whilst adult great-spotteds always have a black cap and a black cheek stripe.

The green woodpecker will already be familiar to many visitors with its green plumage,

Violets in early spring

yellow rump and loud yelping call, known as 'yaffling'. However, in Fontainebleau you should look at each one you see carefully because its close relative, the grey-headed woodpecker, also occurs in the more open parts of the woodland. As its name implies, it has a grey head and lacks the extensive red crown of the green woodpecker.

The real prize of the Forest of Fontainebleau is the black woodpecker. This is Europe's largest woodpecker, the size of a crow, with jet-black plumage.

Although occasionally located by sight alone, the best way to find one is to listen for its far-carrying flutey call, quite unlike any other woodpecker, or its extremely loud drumming.

Woodland Flowers

Springtime in Paris itself is legendary, but it is also, of course, a delightful time to visit the Paris woodlands. Before the leaves are fully formed on the trees, dappled light filters through the canopy to the woodland floor. The spring is the best growing period for most woodland flowers because there is still plenty of light before the canopy shades it out. Many wither and die back by the time summer comes.

Wood sorrel, with its delicate white flowers and shamrock leaves, often forms carpets on the woodland floor with patches of common dog violets adding a splash of mauve and the flowers of wood anemones nodding in the slightest woodland breeze. Large patches of anemones with their large, dissected leaves and striking flowers can give the impression of a well-cared-for garden border plant rather than a wild flower.

In more open areas, particularly in clearings and along tracks,

PEACE AND QUIET

you may come across the showy spikes of early purple orchids with glossy, spotted leaves. This is generally the first orchid to appear in the woods around Paris, and is often in flower in the first week of May. It is followed by many other species later in the year and, in the Forest of Fontainebleau in particular, up to 20 species occur, although many are very local in their distribution.

In the deep shade of beech woods look for the bird's nest orchid, one of the less showy species found in the region, but nevertheless one with a fascinating way of life. This curious straw-coloured plant, which grows up to 1 foot (30cm) tall, has no leaves and is almost entirely lacking in chlorophyll, the pigment which gives plants their green colour.

Woodland Mammals

The forests surrounding the Paris basin were once the hunting preserves of the French nobility. The original quarry animals still survive and the deer are still occasionally hunted.

Deer occur in woods as close to Paris as Versailles, but the best place to see them is in the Forest of Fontainebleau, further south. Red deer are the largest species found in this part of France, the stags with their branched, spiky

---

Highlights of the Woodland Year:

Spring

- Migrant warblers arrive.
- Woodland birds singing to advertise breeding territories.
- Nightingales singing at dusk.
- Woodpeckers excavating nest holes.
- Spring flowers carpet the woodland floor.
- A succession of wild orchids.
- Colourful new growth of leaves.

Summer

- Family parties of birds moving noisily through the trees.
- Sparrowhawks circling over the woodland canopy.
- Butterflies such as speckled wood, purple hairstreak and white admiral appear on the wing.
- Insects such as beetles and flies in abundance.
- Squirrels with young.

Autumn

- The leaves begin to change colour – shades of yellow and brown predominate.
- Berries, fruits and nuts are produced in abundance.
- Squirrels and jays gathering acorns on the woodland floor.
- Colourful fungi appear.
- Deer rutting at the start of the mating season.

Winter

- Woodland birds such as chaffinches form flocks.
- Fieldfares, redwings and bramblings arrive as winter visitors to the woodlands.
- Winter fungi appear.
- Lichens, mosses and ferns seen well with no leaves on the trees.
- Small mammals forage on the ground.

A magnificent red deer stag

antlers. Listen for the loud, cough-like bark with which they signal danger to others.

The smaller fallow deer has beautiful, dappled fur in the summer and the males have broad, flattened antlers. Both fallow and red deer are herd animals and have a distinct rutting season in the autumn. Dominant stags defend a harem of females from intruding males and their loud bellowing calls carry a long way on a misty October morning. Both fallow and red deer produce their young in the late spring. The dappled fawns and calves, as they are respectively known, are well camouflaged against the woodland floor. If you come across one do not touch it – your scent may cause its mother to desert it when she returns.

The smallest deer found in the woods around Paris is the tiny roe deer. Their rutting season is in July and August when their coats are a warm red colour. You might hear their piping and barking calls while on an early morning walk through the woods. By December, when they shed their antlers, their coat has become grey-brown. This blends in with the surrounding vegetation, but when they run they have a conspicuous white patch around the tail.

One of the noisiest of the woodland's inhabitants is the wild boar which forages loudly in the woodland floor and frequently snorts. For all its apparent brashness, it can be difficult to see, crashing off through the undergrowth at the first sign of danger.

Harvest from the Fields and Forests

The French have a passion for fungi. Mushrooms and toadstools of all sorts feature heavily in French cuisine and there are whole markets devoted to them with a vast range of species offered for sale. Of course, if you want the freshest fungi of all, you have to go and pick them yourself and autumn fungus forays are a popular Parisian pursuit in the woods and fields surrounding the capital.

However, identifying some of the choicest species takes considerable skill so for the casual observer perhaps the best advice is to look and admire but do not touch.

Fields and grassland are the traditional site for the field mushroom, the wild ancestor of the most familiar of all edible fungi. However, stately parasol mushrooms, which sometimes grow in large groups, are equally prized. But in terms of weight and size there is nothing to beat the giant puffball which can grow to a size of 2 feet (60cm) in diameter. This species is particularly delicious coated in egg and breadcrumbs and deep-fried. With all fungi it is essential to pick them when they are just at their best. This is certainly the case with the giant puffball. A day or two too late and all you are left with is a giant bag of spores! Woodlands offer a greater variety of mushrooms and toadstools than fields. The 'cep' or penny bun, which has pores instead of gills under its cap, is one of the most popular species in French kitchens and is common under birch trees.

Fungi come in all shapes and sizes. Two of the tastiest are funnel-shaped with gills on the outside. At first glance the horn of plenty is rather dark and unappealing and is certainly difficult to spot amongst the dead leaves on the woodland floor. Since it dries well, it is often kept to flavour stews and soups. The chanterelle looks as good as it tastes – an attractive orange colour with a sharp smell of apricots. Do not expect to find the most famous and most expensive of France's fungi, the truffle, easily. They lie buried deep beneath the soil and require the nose of a trained dog to locate them.

Interesting Peace and Quiet Sites

- Forêt de Fontainebleau – extensive woodland with a wealth of birds and flowers. Something of interest throughout the year.
- Bois de Boulogne – woodland birds and rose gardens of the Parc de Bagatelle.
- Bois de Vincennes – parkland birds and pleasant strolls.
- Forêt de Chantilly – mixed woodland, good for walks.
- Forêt de Rambouillet – mixed woodland, good for walks.
- Forêt de Marly – mixed woodland.
- Forêt de Versailles – especially good for birds. Interesting throughout the year.
- Jardin des Plantes – botanical garden, best in spring and summer.
- Jardin du Luxembourg – parkland.
- Jardin de Tuileries – parkland.

SHOPPING

Parisian women of all ages stand out a mile whether dressed in exclusive *haute couture* or the stylish garb of a student. Their elegant, chic appearance makes most visitors feel their own wardrobe could do with a revamp, so shopping for clothes, or at least accessories, takes on a pressing importance.

Paris shop windows are exhibition pieces in themselves. It is almost impossible to walk past the tempting window displays of the *confiseries, pâtisseries* and *charcuteries* as well as the shops selling perfumes and lingerie. While shopping in Paris *can* cost the earth, if you know where to go it need not be at all expensive. Some salons and boutiques shut on Mondays, although all the large main department stores are open.

The old Les Halles market has been completely transformed into a modern underground shopping centre called the Forum

The Main Areas

Although Paris is not very large, you might like to concentrate your shopping, particularly if you are short of time, on one area. If you want to buy clothes, the most exclusive fashion houses are in the 8e on the Right Bank (*Rive Droite*).

There are, of course, more reasonably priced designer boutiques all over Paris, with a concentration on the Left Bank in and around St-Germain-des-Prés. If you do not mind shopping underground, there are numerous boutiques in the Forum des Halles near Beaubourg. All the main designers are also represented in the Galeries Lafayette.

SHOPPING

Antiques

The equivalent of Sotheby's is Drouot Richelieu at 9 rue Drouot, 9e (11.00 to 18.00, closed Sundays). There are three floors with several salesrooms. Anyone can have a look.

It is also well worth browsing in the beautiful arcaded Le Louvre des Antiquaires (2 place du Palais Royal, 1er) opposite the Louvre, where 250 dealers offer a range of quality antiques from French furniture to jewellery. Open daily from 11.00 to 19.00 (closed Monday all year and Sundays in July and August). Otherwise there are antique shops on the Right Bank; on the Ile St Louis; in the nearby Marais; on the Ile de la Cité and in the rue du Faubourg-Saint-Honoré in the 8e. And on the Left Bank, in the rue du Bac 7e, the rue Jacob 6e, and around the rue de l'Université 7e.

You can buy old prints and postcards from the booksellers on the *quais* along the banks of the Seine.

Department Stores

Most of the department stores are on the Right Bank near the Opéra and the Hôtel de Ville. Au Bon Marché is on the Left. Many of the stores are spread over several buildings.

Galeries Lafayette, 40 boulevard Haussmann, 9e, is possibly the most up-market and sophisticated (there is also a branch in the Montparnasse Shopping Centre). Both branches have an excellent range of top designer clothes for men, women and children as well as their own labels, good ideas for gifts, jewellery and

kitchen gadgets. There are good views of Paris from the top-floor roof terrace.

Printemps, at 64 boulevard Haussmann 9e, claims to be the most Parisian – it is over 100 years old. The perfume hall is vast, and the store devotes a large amount of space to design and home furnishings. It too has excellent views from the roof terrace (with a multi-nationality self-service restaurant under the stained-glass dome) on the top floor. There are other branches. Two of the oldest department stores are **Au Bon Marché** in the rue du Bac/rue de Sèvres, 7e on the Left Bank (worth visiting for its selection of perfumes, linens and sensible household equipment) and **La Samaritaine** on the rue de Rivoli and rue de la

Galeries Lafayette is one of several department stores on the Right Bank

Monnaie in the 1er, a vast store that claims to sell virtually everything from maids' uniforms to pets. Their roof terrace bar on the 10th floor of Magasin 2 is open from April to September. The **Bazar de l'Hôtel de Ville** further down the rue de Rivoli, 4e is also huge and not terribly interesting for visitors as its main claim to fame is 'do-it-yourself', though they do open until 22.00 on Wednesdays if you fancy some late night shopping.

Aux Trois Quartiers, in the boulevard de la Madeleine, 1er is a less exciting alternative. Many department stores also have a food section.

Prisunic (avenue des Champs-Elysées, 8e and other branches) or the first floor of **Monoprix** next to Printemps in boulevard Haussmann are both good for take-home shopping: wine, French mustard, cheese, coffee,

chocolate, perhaps a garlic press. Monoprix and Prisunic are also the cheapest places to buy things for children, household items, underwear, accessories and costume jewellery.

Tax: If you spend over a certain amount, you can get a tax refund of 13 or 18 per cent which is forwarded to your home address if you keep all the relevant receipts (see **Tax Refund** page 118) and get the forms stamped at Customs.

Opening hours: Department stores open from 09.30 until 18.30 and one or two nights for late night shopping (until 21.00 or 22.00). If you get stuck there are information desks in most of them and generally more helpful assistants than in some of the smaller boutiques.

Fashion

Haute couture and famous designer labels (Chanel, Cardin, Balmain, Dior and the like) can be found in the 8e and the 1er *arrondissements,* particularly along the avenue Montaigne and the lower end of the rue du Faubourg-St-Honoré near the Elysée Palace. The avenue Victor Hugo and the avenue Marceau in the 16e also have exclusive salons. While prices for complete outfits can be astronomical, you can pick up reasonably priced accessories. For *prêt à porter* (off-the-peg items) the Left Bank is full of fashion boutiques. Most are around St-Germain-des-Prés (rue de Sèvres, rue du Cherche-Midi, rue de Grenelle and the place Saint-Sulpice).

The Marais is quieter. New designers show their wares in discreet boutiques under

SHOPPING

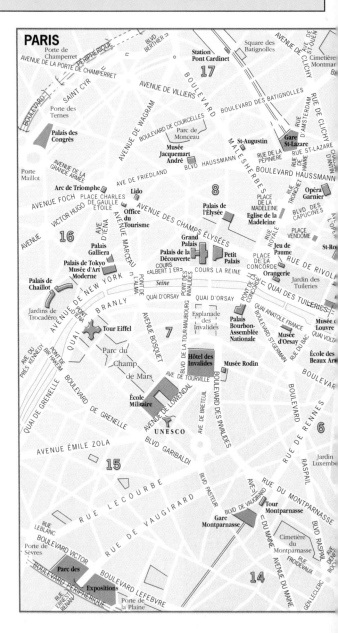

PARIS

Porte de Champerret
AVENUE DE LA PORTE DE CHAMPERRET
BLVD BERTHIER
PÉRIPHÉRIQUE

Square des Batignolles
AVENUE DE CLICHY
AVENUE DE ST-OUEN
Cimetière Montmar

Station Pont Cardinet
17

SAINT CYR
AVENUE DE VILLIERS
BOULEVARD
RUE DE CLICHY

Porte des Ternes
AVENUE DE WAGRAM
BOULEVARD DES BATIGNOLLES
RUE D'AMSTERDAM

Palais des Congrès
BOULEVARD DE COURCELLES
Parc de Monceau
St-Augustin
Gare St-Lazare
RUE DE LA PÉPINIÈRE
RUE ST-LAZARE
RUE DU HAVRE
RUE D'ANTIN

Porte Maillot
AVENUE DE LA GRANDE ARMÉE
AVENUE DE FRIEDLAND
Musée Jacquemart André
BLVD HAUSSMANN
BOULEVARD HAUSSMANN

Arc de Triomphe
PLACE CHARLES DE GAULLE ÉTOILE
Lido
8
Opéra Garnier

AVENUE FOCH
VICTOR HUGO
AVENUE DES CHAMPS ÉLYSÉES
Office du Tourisme
Palais de l'Élysée
PLACE DE LA MADELEINE
Eglise de la Madeleine
BLVD DES CAPUCINES

AVENUE
16
AVE D'IÉNA
AVENUE MARCEAU
Grand Palais
Palais de la Découverte
Petit Palais
PLACE ROYALE
PLACE VENDÔME
St-Ro

Palais Galliera
Palais de Tokyo
Musée d'Art Moderne
COURS ALBERT 1 ER
COURS LA REINE
PLACE DE LA CONCORDE
Jeu de Paume
Orangerie
RUE DE RIVOLI

Palais de Chaillot
PONT DE L'ALMA
Seine
QUAI D'ORSAY
PONT DE LA CONCORDE
Jardin des Tuileries
QUAI DES TUILERIES
Musée du Louvre

Jardins de Trocadéro
RUE DE NEW YORK
BRANLY
QUAI D'ORSAY
QUAI ANATOLE FRANCE
QUAI VOLT

AVE DU PRÉS KENNEDY
PONT DE BIR HAKEIM
PONT D'IÉNA
QUAI
Tour Eiffel
AVENUE BOSQUET
7
Esplanade des Invalides
Palais Bourbon-Assemblée Nationale
Musée d'Orsay
BOULEVARD ST-GERMAIN
RUE DU BAC
École des Beaux Art

Parc du Champ de Mars
BLVD DE LA TOUR-MAUBOURG
Hôtel des Invalides
Musée Rodin
AVE DE TOURVILLE
BOULEVAR

QUAI DE GRENELLE
BOULEVARD DE GRENELLE
École Militaire
AVENUE DE LOWENDAL
AVE DE BRETEUIL
BOULEVARD DES INVALIDES
BOULEVARD DE RENNES
6

AVENUE ÉMILE ZOLA
UNESCO
BLVD GARIBALDI
RASPAIL
Jardin Luxemb

RUE LECOURBE
15
BLVD PASTEUR
RUE DU MONTPARNASSE
BLVD RASPAIL

RUE LEBLANC
BOULEVARD VICTOR
RUE DE VAUGIRARD
AVE D
BLVD DE VAUGIRARD
Tour Montparnasse
RUE DU MAINE

Porte de Sèvres
Parc des Expositions
BOULEVARD PÉRIPHÉRIQUE
BOULEVARD LEFEBVRE
RUE ERNEST RENAN
Gare Montparnasse
Cimetière du Montparnasse
AVE FROIDEVAUX
RUE DENFER
GEN. LECLERC

Porte de la Plaine
14
AVENUE DU MAINE

59

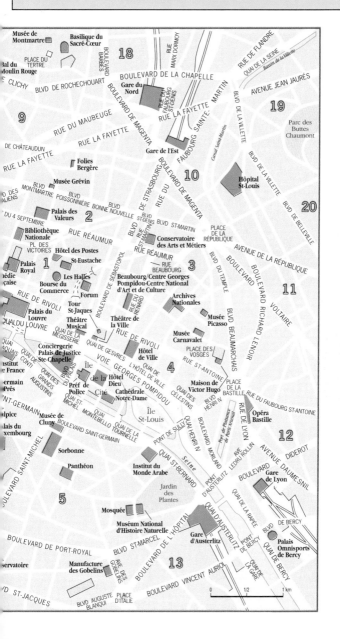

Musée de Montmartre
Basilique du Sacré-Cœur
PLACE DU TERTRE
Bal du Moulin Rouge
CLICHY
BOULEVARD BARBÈS
RUE MARX DORMOY
RUE DE FLANDRE
QUAI DE LA SEINE
Bassin de la Villette
AVENUE JEAN JAURÈS
18
BOULEVARD DE LA CHAPELLE
BLVD DE ROCHECHOUART
BOULEVARD DE MAGENTA
Gare du Nord
RUE DU FAUBOURG ST-DENIS
RUE LA FAYETTE
FAUBOURG SAINTE-MARTIN
BLVD DE LA VILLETTE
19
Parc des Buttes Chaumont
9
RUE DU MAUBEUGE
RUE LA FAYETTE
Canal Saint-Martin
DE CHÂTEAUDUN
RUE LA FAYETTE
Gare de l'Est
10
BLVD DE LA VILLETTE
Hôpital St-Louis
20
Folies Bergère
Musée Grévin
BLVD MONTMARTRE
POISSONNIÈRE
BLVD
BONNE NOUVELLE
BLVD
BOULEVARD DE STRASBOURG
RUE DU FAUBOURG ST-DENIS
BOULEVARD DE MAGENTA
BLVD DE BELLEVILLE
DES ITALIENS
DU 4 SEPTEMBRE
Palais des Valeurs
2
BLVD ST-DENIS
BLVD ST-MARTIN
Bibliothèque Nationale
RUE RÉAUMUR
RUE ST-MARTIN
Conservatoire des Arts et Métiers
PLACE DE LA RÉPUBLIQUE
AVENUE DE LA RÉPUBLIQUE
PL. DES VICTOIRES
Hôtel des Postes
St-Eustache
RUE RÉAUMUR
Palais Royal
1
RUE BEAUBOURG
3
BOULEVARD DE SÉBASTOPOL
RUE DU TEMPLE
BOULEVARD
BOULEVARD VOLTAIRE
BOULEVARD RICHARD LENOIR
médie çaise
Les Halles
Bourse du Commerce
Forum
Beaubourg/Centre Georges Pompidou-Centre National d'Art et de Culture
Archives Nationales
11
RUE DE RIVOLI
Palais du Louvre
Tour St-Jacques
Théâtre Musical
RUE DU RENARD
Théâtre de la Ville
Musée Picasso
BLVD BEAUMARCHAIS
QUAI DU LOUVRE
QUAI DE LA MÉGISSERIE
QUAI DE GESVRES
RUE DE RIVOLI
Musée Carnavalet
QUAI
AQUAIS CONTI
Conciergerie
Palais de Justice Ste-Chapelle
QUAI DES GRANDS AUGUSTINS
BLVD DU PALAIS
Île de la Cité
Hôtel de Ville
RUE DE L'HÔTEL DE VILLE
4
QUAI DE L'HÔTEL DE VILLE
QUAI DES CÉLESTINS
PLACE DES VOSGES
RUE ST-ANTOINE
Maison de Victor Hugo
PLACE DE LA BASTILLE
RUE DU FAUBOURG ST-ANTOINE
Institut e France
Hôtel Dieu
Préf de Police
Cité
QUAI ST-MICHEL
germain
Près
NT-GERMAIN
Cathédrale Notre-Dame
Île St-Louis
QUAI MONTEBELLO
QUAI DE LA TOURNELLE
PONT DE SULLY
BOULEVARD MORLAND
QUAI HENRI IV
Port de Plaisance de Paris-Arsenal
BLVD HENRI IV
Opéra Bastille
12
lpice
Musée de Cluny
BOULEVARD SAINT-GERMAIN
Sorbonne
BOULEVARD SAINT-MICHEL
Panthéon
Institut du Monde Arabe
QUAI ST-BERNARD
Jardin des Plantes
Seine
PONT D'AUSTERLITZ
AVE LEDRU ROLLIN
RUE DE LYON
AVENUE DAUMESNIL
AVENUE DIDEROT
BOULEVARD
Gare de Lyon
alais du xembourg
5
QUAI DE LA RAPÉE
QUAI DE LA GARE
PONT DE BERCY
BLVD DE BERCY
Mosquée
Muséum National d'Histoire Naturelle
Gare d'Austerlitz
QUAI D'AUSTERLITZ
Palais Omnisports de Bercy
BOULEVARD DE PORT-ROYAL
BLVD ST-MARCEL
BOULEVARD DE L'HÔPITAL
13
servatoire
Manufacture des Gobelins
AVE DES GOBELINS
PLACE D'ITALIE
BOULEVARD VINCENT AURIOL
BLVD AUGUSTE BLANQUI
D ST-JACQUES
0   1/2   1 km

SHOPPING

awnings around the place des Victoires (there is even a Kenzo for kids within the main shop) and others. Jean Paul Gaultier has his showpiece in the arcaded *passage* in the rue Vivienne, 2e. There are numerous boutiques in the vast Forum des Halles. The best place of all to shop for clothes is on the designer or own collection floors of Galeries Lafayette or Printemps.
Discounts Fashion would not be fashion in Paris if it did not date quickly. You can pick up last year's designer labels discounted by up to 50 per cent by shopping in the discount shops. Do not expect personal service, changing rooms or to be able to take anything back if you change your mind. Streets to look for include: the rue Saint-Placide, 6e (Moda Soldes sell discounted shoes); the rue Saint-Dominique, 7e (Stock Sacs sell discounted bags). At 65 rue

Hédiard and Fauchon, in the place de la Madeleine, should not be missed by food lovers

Montmartre, 9e, Mendes sell St Laurent cast-offs. Look for shops with *Stock* in the name (including Cacharel and Dorothée Bis) along the rue d'Alésia, 14e. If you do not mind crowds and are prepared to sort through piles of rubbish, there are also bargains at Tati (branches 4–30 boulevard Rochechouart, 18e; 140 rue de Rennes, 6e; 13 place de la République, 11e). There is a clothes market in the 3e in the Carreau du Temple.

Food
If you love food a walk around the place de la Madeleine, 8e will be a mouth-watering experience. Fauchon at number 26 is the jewel in the crown, the world famous *épicier* (grocer) where you can buy everything

from fresh *foie gras* to caviar, as well as olive oil, mustards, cheeses and exquisitely prepared dishes to take away from dressed crab to colourful terrines. Upstairs there are biscuits and hundreds of teas, all in attractive tins. Everything at Fauchon is packaged up beautifully.

Hédiard at number 21 opposite is tiny by comparison but has a wonderful display of exotic fruits under a palm tree. Next to Hédiard is the Maison de la Truffe (number 19) for fresh truffles, then comes a little shop that sells nothing but cheese, with a couple of tiny tables neatly laid so you can sample as many as you like. At number 17 the Caviar Kaspia specialises in caviar (you can eat it in the restaurant upstairs), and just in

case by this time you are getting thirsty, almost next door there is a branch of the famous L'Ecluse wine bar.

Of course, there are also numerous *charcuteries, fromageries, pâtisseries* all over Paris as well as shops specialising in specific food items from caviar to snails. For hand-made chocolate try Lenotre, 44 rue de Bac, 7e, or 3 rue du Havre, 9e, or the Maison du Chocolat, 225 rue du Faubourg-St-Honoré, 8e. The best ice cream in Paris is from Berthillon, 31 rue St-Louis-en-L'Ile. Ingenious flavours. Poilâne, 8 rue du Cherche-Midi, 6e, is possibly the most famous bread shop in France. They specialise in amazing shapes. At Androuet, 41 rue d'Amsterdam, 8e you can try the famous cheeses for yourself (at lunchtime or in the evening) as well as buy regional cheeses in pristine condition from all over France.

Flo Prestige, 42 place du Marché-Saint-Honoré, 1er, sells portions of gourmet food.

Gifts, Jewellery and Accessories
Paris is full of exclusive shops selling quality gifts and accessories, although the main stores are much better value. For perfumes all the major houses – Guerlain, Balmain, Lancôme – have shops, many in the Champs-Elysées, 8e or the place Vendôme, 1er. You will also see shops offering duty-free prices, especially in the avenue de l'Opéra and the Champs-Elysées, but the airport may still be cheaper.

SHOPPING

The top jewellers – Boucheron, Cartier, Van Cleef & Arpels – are in the place Vendôme. For luggage, Louis Vuitton in the avenue Marceau, 8e is the top designer. For china and crystal the Lalique shop is at 11 rue Royale in the 8e. Any of the *passages* (see pages 63–64) will yield rewarding shops selling unusual items.

Markets

Paris has over 80 permanent markets, covered and uncovered, offering a range of goods from antiques to food, children's toys to pets. The Mairie de Paris publishes a free list which you can get from the tourist office.

Antique Markets: For bric à brac and bigger pieces of furniture you can wade through the miles of junk in one of the huge outdoor markets. Be prepared to bargain, get there early and hang onto your valuables.

The largest flea market, (*marché aux puces*), 4 miles (6km) long with 3,000 stalls, is at the Porte de Clignancourt/Saint Ouen in the 18e (Saturday to Monday). You could also try the Porte de Vanves (avenue Georges Lafenestre and avenue Marc Sangnier in the 14e, Saturday and Sunday).

For clothes the Porte de Montreuil market in the 20e runs from Saturday to Monday.

Birds: The bird and pet market is held on Sundays in the Marché aux Oiseaux in the place Louis-Lépine on the Ile de la Cité, 4e, where they also sell flowers during the rest of the week. You can also see birds and other animals along the quai de la Mégisserie, 1er.

Clothes: the Carreau du Temple in the Marais, 3e just south of the République is open from 09.00 to 19.00 every day except Monday. You can buy antique clothes in the Aligre market, in the place d'Aligre, 12e, daily until 13.00, except Monday (also fruit and vegetables in the neighbouring streets).

Food: there are over 80 food markets in Paris, both uncovered and covered. Among the most lively are: the place Monge, 5e and the streets around the rue Mouffetard; the rue de Buci (6e) and adjoining rue de Seine in St-Germain-des-Prés; Raspail (6e) between the rues du Cherche-Midi and de Rennes; the Charonne near the Bastille in the Ile. Get there early for the still-squirming sea food, the oozing cheeses and the shiny fruit and vegetables that look as if each piece has been individually polished.

Buy plaits of garlic and handfuls of herbs to take home or just savour the smells.

Buy *saucisson*, *salami*, or a waxy cardboard box of a divine seafood salad, a piece of cheese, a crisp *baguette*, and a bottle of wine and you have all the ingredients for a wonderful French picnic. Or just take some mouth-watering photos. Most stalls shut up shop at lunchtime and then open again from 16.00 until about 19.30. Prices are fixed so do not try and bargain.

Prints: both banks of the River Seine are lined with *quais* where prints and second-hand books are sold. Look for the quais du Louvre, de la

Mégisserie ler, quais des Grands Augustins, de Conti et Malaquais in the 6e.

Flowers: the place Louis-Lépine on the Ile de la Cité (Monday to Saturday); the place de la Madeleine, 8e (Tuesday to Sunday); or the place des Ternes, 17e (not Monday).

Stamps: the main stamp market is under the trees between the avenue Gabriel and the avenue de Marigny just off the Champs-Elysées, 8e, Thursdays, Saturdays and Sundays from 10.00 to 19.00.

The market in the place Louis-Lépine on the Ile de la Cité sells birds and pets on Sundays

Les Passages

Paris has nearly 100 *passages*, glass-domed arcades down which the early 18th- and 19th-century Parisians could browse without getting wet; the equivalent of the modern shopping mall, with family-run firms selling everything from chops to china. Some have been renovated and now house travel agents, designer boutiques and hairdressers, others are delightfully dilapidated with carved shop fronts, painted ceilings and marble counters. Behind even the most crumbling façades are some of Paris's most interesting shops, many of them family firms going back generations. Most are in the 1er and 2e, although there are others in the 9e and 10e.

The Galerie Vivienne (various entrances, one at 4 rue des Petits-Champs, 2e) is one of the most splendid architecturally with wrought-iron work, mosaic tiles and high roof with bas reliefs. Leading off it is the Galerie Colbert where Jean Paul Gaultier has his showroom (with fashion shows on videos under glass bubbles on the floor).

The rather grand copper and mahogany fronted Galerie Véro-Dodat built by two butchers in 1824 is at 19 rue Jean-Jacques Rousseau, 1er. Behind the wooden pillars and gleaming brass doors, there are numerous interesting shops, selling musical instruments, antiques, and antiquarian books. There is also a tiny, intimate restaurant, the Véro Dodat on two floors (closed Sunday and Monday lunch). Also worth a look are the three linked *passages*: des Panoramas, Jouffroy and Verdeau at boulevard Montmartre, 2e.

Shopping Centres

The old Les Halles market is now replaced by the glass and chrome shell of the underground **Forum des Halles**, 1–7 rue Pierre-Lescot, 1er. It is the largest pedestrian shopping area in Europe, with four levels of shops, discos, banks, restaurants and cinemas reached by escalators.

The place is full of boutiques and designer furniture shops, art galleries and cafés. If you need to cool off in a hurry, there is an indoor swimming pool at the Nouveau Forum opposite the church of St-Eustache.

The **Palais des Congrès** shopping centre (2 place de la Porte Maillot, 17e) is inside the convention building: a vast complex with shops, restaurants, cinemas and an air terminal. The Concorde Lafayette hotel (1,000 rooms) is also part of the complex.

Montparnasse, 14e, between the rue de L'Arrivée and the rue du Départ (next to the Air France terminal), is now the heart of the business area of Paris, dominated by the 679-foot (207m) Montparnasse Tower, which has one of the best views of the city from the observatory on the 56th floor. The commercial/shopping centre is on eight levels, six of them underground with the upper three floors devoted to fashion shops, restaurants and cafés (including a branch of Galeries Lafayette). The rest includes a vast car park and a sports centre with public swimming pool.

La Défence

Outside the Périphérique, but reachable by Métro, RER and bus, the new development at La Défence is primarily a business district with a skyline of towering offices, but there is also a big shopping centre. The impressive new Grande Arche is at the western end of the pedestrian esplanade. This 35-storey office block in the shape of a hollow cube offers superb views from the roof.

FOOD AND DRINK

Eating Out

Do not assume that just because you are in Paris wherever you eat the food will be good, nor will it even necessarily be French. The city is full of mediocre restaurants of every nationality, as well as some of the very best restaurants in the world. And the good ones are not always expensive. Although you can join the queues at one of the many brasseries in the capital, or take your chances at one of the many cheap bistros, the very best restaurants (and not necessarily the most expensive) get booked up and need reserving well in advance.

What you might find disappointing if you are planning a weekend in the city is that many of these restaurants close at weekends. And if you are visiting in July or August they may well be shut for the entire month for their holidays. Many restaurants serve a fixed price menu (especially at lunchtime), which can even make the most expensive restaurants in Paris manageable. This might include three or four courses, with a number of choices within each. Wine is also sometimes included. Service and tax are always included so there is no need to leave a tip. Lunchtime is always busy in a good Parisian restaurant. They eat early with

Whenever possible Parisians sit out in the open air, especially on the Left Bank around St-Michel

FOOD AND DRINK

last orders well before 14.30 but then if you want a drink and a snack mid-afternoon you can go to a café or *salon de thé*. In the evening last orders in some restaurants may be 21.30 or 22.00. Many brasseries open until one or two in the morning and most are open at weekends. Your best guide to where to get the best food is the red *Michelin Paris* or the *Gault Millau* for Paris, a bible of a book, which describes restaurants in detail, though unfortunately only in French.

For cheap restaurants, *Paupers' Paris* by Miles Turner (Pan) has a good selection.

The following is a selection of restaurants in different categories in central areas:

Brasseries

Brasseries tend to be big, noisy and bustling. The food is usually good, many brasseries have displays of seafood outside, and also serve Alsatian specialities like sauerkraut. The service is fast, and the clientele mixed. Many serve meals after midnight and are open every day. Because of their size you are more likely to get a table without a reservation though you will probably have to queue. The following are among those with the best food and/or the most character:

Le Boeuf sur le Toit, 34 rue du Colisée, 8e (tel: 43 59 83 80). Art Deco and Art Nouveau decor, seafood on display in the outer courtyard. Smart. Good reasonably priced food. Open daily until 02.00.

Bofinger, 5 rue de la Bastille, 4e (tel: 42 72 87 82). Near the new Opera house, very popular and open every day until 01.00. One of the very first brasseries, with ornate Belle Epoque decor and gilt mirrors, seats 300 in several different areas. They serve vast platters of seafood, excellent *bouillabaisse* and Alsatian specialities.

Brasserie Flo, 7 cour des Petites-Ecuries, 10e (tel: 47 70 13 59). Wonderful display of still squirming seafood outside, turn-of-the-century decor inside. Worth the trip to get there and the queue to get in. Open every day until 01.30.

Brasserie Lipp, 151 boulevard St-Germain, 6e (tel: 45 48 53 91). Opposite the famous cafés de Flore and Les Deux Magots. Up-market meeting place. Good food, serious meals rather than snacks. On two floors. They turn away people they do not like the look of and put doubtfuls on the first floor. Open until 02.00. Not cheap.

Brasserie Saint-Benoît, 26 rue Saint-Benoît, 6e (tel: 45 48 29 66). Very cheap traditional brasserie in St-Germain, especially if you stick to the set menus. Outside terrace. Closed Sunday in winter. Open until midnight.

Chez Jenny, 39 boulevard du Temple, 3e (tel: 42 74 75 75). Popular brasserie serving Alsatian food of the *choucroute* variety as well as substantial French dishes. Seats 625 in five separate rooms. Still going strong after 30 years. Open every day until 01.00.

La Coupole, 102 boulevard du Montparnasse, 14e (tel: 43 20 14 20). One of Paris' best-known and loved brasseries, newly renovated. An enormous 1930s-

style meeting place (with a ballroom for tea dances downstairs) once popular with intellectuals.
Run by the people who own Brasserie Flo, Chez Julien and Terminus Nord. Open until 02.00. Set in a good location to combine with a climb up the Montparnasse Tower.
Terminus Nord, 23 rue de Dunkerque, 10e (tel: 42 85 05 15). Opposite the station (there are two, this is the one with a display of seafood outside). If you have just come in by train, an excellent place to get acclimatised. Excellent food (also drinks *only*). A good taste of things to come. Open every day until 00.30.
Vaudeville, 29 rue Vivienne, 2e (tel: 40 20 04 62). Open until 01.30 every day. Near the Bourse, so popular with city slickers at lunchtime. 1920s decor. Good seafood, lively and reasonably priced.

Brasseries serve the best seafood – here a mouthwatering display at the Terminus Nord

Drugstores
Drugstores do not sell drugs (at least not openly) but drinks, meals, books, clothes and souvenirs. They tend to open until late, and attract disorientated visitors and Paris youngsters. An inexpensive place to eat steak, ice-cream and hamburgers. One of the most popular is at the top of the Champs-Elysées, **Publicis Champs-Elysées** at number 133. There is another, the **Publicis Saint-Germain**, next to Brasserie Lipp at 149 boulevard St-Germain. They are good places to arrange to meet someone, to use the phone, toilet etc. Others include:
Le Drugstorian, 1 avenue Matignon, 8e
New Store, 63 Champs-Elysées, 8e
Pub Renault, 53 Champs-Elysées, 8e

FOOD AND DRINK

Ethnic Food/Snacks and Take-Aways (*casse-croute*)

Most of the department stores have reasonably priced snack bars and restaurants, as do many of the museums. Some snack bars, especially those selling ethnic food may be open 24 hours. If you have no time to sit down, you can buy a *crêpe* from one of the *crêperie* stands, a thin pancake made in front of you on a flat, black iron ring and stuffed full of jam or other concoctions. You could also try a *croque monsieur* (toasted ham and cheese sandwich) or a *croque madame* (toasted cheese and ham with a fried egg), plus various varieties of *sandwich*. *Charcuteries/traiteurs* are a good source of snacks; they will usually stuff a *baguette* full of salami and sell wonderful salads in waxy containers for you to take away. A plastic knife and fork will come in handy as they are sometimes not supplied and you could have a messy grapple with the ingredients. Cafés and *salons de thé* serve snacks. You may see an *assiette anglaise* on the menu (plate of mixed cold meats). Most places serve omelettes.

There is a concentration of ethnic take-aways in the Latin Quarter in the rue de la Huchette, 5e and in the rue Mouffetard among others. The stalls sell Moroccan, Greek, Middle Eastern, Italian,

Jo Goldenberg restaurant and delicatessen in the Marais

American and French
specialities. You can get Russian
take-aways in the Marais or, if
your imagination runs no further
there are branches of
McDonalds and a Burger King in
the Champs-Elysées.
Ethnic restaurants include:
Japanese: Le Yamato in the
Hôtel Méridien (81 boulevard
Gouvion-St-Cyr, 17e) and **Nikko
Benkay** in the Hôtel Nikko (61
quai de Grenelle, 15e) both have
excellent Japanese restaurants.
Jewish: Jo Goldenberg, 7 rue
des Rosiers, 4e, (tel: 48 87 20
16), serves everything from
chicken soup to chopped liver,
plus a take-away deli bar. Open
on Saturdays. Also at 69 avenue
de Wagram, 17e.
Mexican: the trendy **Café
Pacifico**, 50 boulevard du
Montparnasse, 15e (tel: 45 48 63
87), serves a Mexican brunch,
with band, on a Sunday.
North African: Trois Horloges,
73 rue Brancion, 15e (tel: 48 28
24 08), *bouillabaisse. couscous*
and other Franco/Algerian
specialities. Closed Tuesday
lunch and Monday.
Russian: Dominique, 19 rue
Bréa, 6e (tel: 43 27 08 80).
Borscht and caviar either to take
away or eat there. Reasonable
prices. Or try the fashionable **La
Tchaika** (closed Sundays), 7 rue
de Lappe, 11e near the Bastille
(tel: 47 00 73 61) or **Datcha
Lydie**, 7 rue Dupleix, 15e (tel: 45
66 67 77). Closed Wednesday.
Vietnamese: Tan Dinh, 60 rue
de Verneuil, 7e (tel: 45 44 04 84).
Highly rated restaurant serving
sophisticated Vietnamese
cuisine. Closed Sunday.
If you cannot make up your mind
which nationality you want to

sample, the **Savannah Café** 27
rue Descartes, 5e (tel: 43 29 45
77) offers food from around the
world.
Otherwise there are Korean,
Indian, Brazilian, Italian,
Scandinavian, Turkish, Dutch,
American and English
possibilities. The English-
language *Passion* magazine
(published every two months)
lists many of them and the red
Michelin guide singles out the
best.

French Restaurants – Cheap
You will see *Les Selfs*, or self-
service restaurants, all over the
city. You do not need to speak
the language as the food is
displayed on counters and there
are special daily dishes to
choose from. Cheap, cheerful
and quick once you get past the
lunchtime queues. Several of the
department stores have self-
service restaurants including
Monoprix in the avenue de
l'Opéra, 1er, Printemps, which
offers counters of food of various
nationalities under the stained-
glass dome and Galeries
Lafayette in boulevard
Haussmann. From the roof
terrace on the 10th floor of
Magasin 2 of La Samaritaine in
the rue de la Monnaie there are
good views. You can also buy
snacks in galleries and
museums. Few cheap
restaurants take bookings, so
turn up early or be prepared to
queue.
Here is a short selection of
restaurants if you are on a tight
budget.
Chartier, 7 rue du Faubourg
Montmartre, 9e. Revolving doors
lead to huge soup kitchen with

FOOD AND DRINK

1920s decor, mirrors, shared tables and queues for the food which is excellent value. Closes at 21.30. Open every day.
Le Drouet, 103 rue de Richelieu, 2e. Owned by the same people as Chartier and similar. Open every day. Near the large department stores and the Opéra.
Restaurant du Grand Cerf, passage du Grand Cerf, 2e (off the rue Saint-Denis). Noisy, busy and very cheap serving Spanish and French dishes up until 21.30.
La Canaille, 4 rue Crillon, 4e. Near the port by the Bastille. Popular with students. Closed weekends.
Le Polidor, 41 rue Monsieur-le-Prince, 6e. Famous cheap restaurant, some 50 years old with good food and shared tables. James Joyce used to like it.
Le Trumilou, 84 quai de l'Hôtel-de-Ville, 4e. Small; bright, unpretentious, hundred-year-old restaurant and bar, fresh flowers and pretty crockery. Very cheap set menus, views of Notre-Dame. Closed Mondays.

French Restaurants – Reasonable
Prices soon add up if you order *à la carte*, but stick to the set menu and the house wine (carafe) in some of the places listed below and your bill should still be considerably less than the equivalent meal in London or New York.
Ambassade d'Auvergne, 22 rue du Grenier St-Lazare, 3e (tel: 42 72 31 22). Smart, long-established restaurant near Les Halles, serving somewhat hearty regional recipes of the

Auvergne. *Plats de Saison* good value. Open every day.
La Cagouille, 10 place Brancusi, 14e (tel: 43 22 09 01). Well known for its fish and excellent value. Near the Montparnasse Tower. Noted for its collection of Cognacs and food from the same region. Closed Sunday and Monday.
Chez Quinson, 5 place Etienne-Pernet, 15e (tel: 45 32 48 54). Not right in the centre but worth a visit if you like *bouillabaisse* and food from Provence. Closed Sunday and Monday. Last orders 21.30.
Dodin-Bouffant, 25 rue Frédéric Sauton, 5e (tel: 43 25 25 14). Big, popular, old-fashioned, unpretentious place on two floors with more atmosphere downstairs than up. Hearty portions. Well known for its raspberry soufflé. Good value for money. Closed Sunday in

The temptations of a pâtisserie...

August.
Chez Pauline, 5 rue Villedo, 1er (tel: 42 96 20 70). Highly rated intimate restaurant on two floors, serving classical French cuisine in a formal setting. Closed Saturday evening and Sunday.
Au Pied de Cochon, 6 rue Coquillière, 1er (tel: 42 36 11 75). Famous old Les Halles restaurant that used to be packed with market traders. Open all day and night for dishes like onion soup, oysters and pig's trotters.
Pharamond, 24 rue de la Grande-Truanderie, 1er (tel: 42 33 06 72). Closed Monday lunch and Sunday, mid-July to mid-August. Famous turn-of-the-century restaurant of Les Halles, serving *tripes à la mode de Caen*.
Le Récamier, 4 rue Récamier, 7e (tel: 45 48 86 58). Intimate, first-class food. Closed Sunday.

French Restaurants – Expensive

You can spend the earth in one of the best restaurants in Paris but the sumptuous settings of some of these restaurants are almost worth paying for in themselves. The following are among the very best, regularly scooping Michelin rosettes.
Les Ambassadeurs, Hotel de Crillon, 10 place de la Concorde, 8e (tel: 42 65 24 24). One of the most sumptuous dining rooms in Paris. Palatial 18th-century decor, chandeliers, mirrors and marble, plus terrace overlooking the place de la Concorde. Outstanding kitchen with simple dishes as well as elaborate ones.
L'Ambroisie, 9 place des Vosges, 4e (tel: 42 78 51 45). Tiny, sophisticated restaurant with superb cooking, in an old silversmith's shop under the arcades in the heart of the Marais. Closed Sunday and Monday lunchtime.
Jamin, 32 rue de Longchamp, 16e (tel: 47 27 12 27). Small restaurant well known for the creativity and inventiveness of its highly acclaimed chef. Modern French cuisine using the very best ingredients from all over France. The fixed priced menu is excellent value. Closed Saturday and Sunday.
Le Jules Verne, 2nd floor, south pillar, Eiffel Tower, 7e (tel: 45 55 61 44). Wonderful views, and surprisingly good food. Has its own private lift. Attracts business people and birthday parties. Piano bar, but only with reservations, after 22.30 at night.
Lucas-Carton, 9 place de la Madeleine, 8e (tel: 42 65 22 90). Old-established and very

FOOD AND DRINK

expensive top restaurant with art nouveau decor. Closed Saturday and Sunday.

Taillevent, 15 rue Lamennais, 8e (tel: 45 63 39 94). Another outstanding restaurant, some rate it the best in Paris, so much so that tables have to be reserved months in advance. Spacious, mansion-like restaurant with a club-like atmosphere, wood-panelled rooms and crystal chandeliers. Closed Saturday and Sunday.

Where to Drink

Bars and Cafés

Paris is crammed full of bars and cafés: dingy, smoky, deafeningly noisy bars where everyone stands at a narrow chrome counter; bars with pinball machines and adjacent restaurants; trendy basement bars with pot plants, designer furniture and jazz musicians; old fashioned piano bars in top hotels like the de Crillon; book shop bars; museum and art gallery bars and, of course, the famous bars on the Left Bank, the regular watering-holes of intellectuals from Sartre to Hemingway.

The first thing you should know is that it is cheaper to stand up at the bar than to sit down at a table, where a service charge will be added to your bill. Also, that bars on the main thoroughfares (Champs-Elysées, rue du Rivoli, rue du Faubourg-St-Honoré, and the boulevards St-Germain and St-Michel among them), as well as in places like Beaubourg, around the Opéra and in the main squares, charge a lot more for their drinks than those in side streets just around the corner.

The Café de Flore, as popular with Parisians as visitors, was patronised by Picasso

You can sit outside, or under a glass roof, at those typical round tables that are barely big enough for the drinks, and people-watch. Almost all bars serve snacks and sandwiches of some kind. If you are a beer drinker and want to save money, ask for *un demi* or *une pression*, otherwise you will get a large glass or the more expensive bottled variety. Beer is cheaper than mineral water. Many bars stay open until 02.00. Paris also has its fair share of English-style pubs and American cocktail bars and wine bars where wine is taken seriously and sold by the glass.

The following bars and cafés are among the most famous (and some of the most expensive) in the city.

Café Beaubourg, 45 rue St-Merri, 4e. Similar style to the Café Costes but less frenetic. Open until 02.00.

Café Costes, 6 rue Berger, ler. Very trendy, noisy, crowded and stylish. A modern version of the Grand Café designed to last 100 years! Open until 02.00.

Café de Flore, 172 boulevard St-Germain, 6e. A Left Bank café/brasserie much loved by Picasso, Camus and Simone de Beauvoir. You can sit outside. Open every day until 01.30.

La Coupole, 102 boulevard du Montparnasse, 14e. Huge *brasserie* and American bar, newly re-vamped, popular with intellectuals past and present.

Les Deux Magots, 170 boulevard St-Germain, 6e. The famous café where Sartre watched the girls go by for inspiration. Still a meeting place with tables spilling out onto the pavement and views of St-Germain-des-Prés. Try the hot chocolate or the numerous brands of whisky. Also a brasserie. Open until 02.00 every day.

L'Entre-Pôts, 14 rue de Charonne, 11e. Heart of the Bastille nightlife area. Sophisticated bar with cool modern decor and exotic cocktails.

Le Grand Café Capucines, 4 boulevard des Capucines, 9e. Very grand large restaurant/café near the Opéra, in the Belle Epoque style, open day and all night.

Harry's Bar, 5 rue Daunou, 2e. An American bar where they have been mixing drinks for people like Hemingway since 1921.

Exotic cocktails and piano bar in the basement. Open until 04.00.

Hôtel de Crillon, 10 place de la Concorde, 8e. Plush, elegant setting, in a former palace, with pianist.

Lipp, 151 boulevard St-Germain, 6e. Opposite Café de Flore and Les Deux Magots, making up the famous threesome. More of a brasserie than a café.

Salons de Thé (Tea Shops)
There are plenty of tea shops in Paris, some grand, some tiny. Most of them open from noon until early evening and serve light meals, irresistible cakes and ice creams. Some are in *pâtisseries*. **Fauchon**, for example, at 26 place de la Madeleine, 8e, serve their irresistible cakes at narrow chrome counters.

One of the most famous and oldest (1903) *salons de thé* is **Angelina** in the rue de Rivoli, ler

FOOD AND DRINK

Fanny's tiny tea shop, between the Pont Neuf and the Conciergerie in the place Dauphine

(number 226) near the Louvre, well known for their hot chocolate with whipped cream, as is **Laduré** tea room and *pâtisserie* (16 rue Royale, 8e), an opulent *salon de thé* with Louis XIV decor where they make their own chocolates.

On the Ile de la Cité (4e) you can have a real English tea at **Fanny's**, 20 place Dauphine, a tiny old-fashioned, homely place. There are several tea shops in splendid settings, including: **La Pagode** (52 bis rue de Babylone, 7e), an original Japanese pagoda, now a cinema. You can have tea in the garden whether you see a film or not. The

Moroccan **Café de la Mosquée** (rue Geoffroy-St-Hilaire, 5e), near the Jardin des Plantes, serves mint tea in the mosque itself and on a patio in the garden when it is fine. In the Marais, at 37 rue Vieille du Temple, you can have tea upstairs at **Christhiey Paris** in among an eccentric tropical jungle of buddhas, plants and furniture. A pianist plays downstairs. You can also have an English tea in **W H Smith's Bookshop** at 248 rue de Rivoli. The best ice cream in Paris is from **Berthillon's** at 31 rue St-Louis-en-l'Isle, 4e.

Wine Bars

Wine bars are expensive and take their wines seriously. A glass can cost as much as a bottle in a brasserie. Although you do not usually go to eat, they also serve simple dishes – perhaps some salami or cheese or a slice of *foie gras*. The Paris wine bar scene more or less began with the British owned **Willi's** (13 rue des Petits-Champs, ler), which also serves light meals, as does Le Rouge Gorge (8 rue St Paul, 4e) in the Marais district. There is also the **Blue Fox** (25 rue Royale, 8e) and **Le Petit Bacchus** (13 rue du Cherche-Midi, 6e). All are trendy watering-holes and the staff speak English so you will get good advice on what to drink. Look for bars in the **L'Ecluse** chain. Many wine bars shut at weekends.

Cheese and Wine

Virtually everyone spending time in Paris is going to want to sample the wine; after all, it's one of the best things about France! A good deal of rubbish is talked about wine, and that tends to cloud the fact that drinking it is a pleasure, and a pleasure that can become more and more fascinating as you discover the subtleties of different kinds. So, try a variety, and why not try them with some of the speciality cheeses of the area around Paris?

Cheese

France is the largest producer of cheese in the world after the US, with each region producing its own speciality. The Ile de France, the area around Paris, produces a number of cheeses of which the most famous is the brie de Meaux, round and flat and covered in a white mould, voted 'King of Cheeses' in 1815 by the 143 negotiators of the Congress of Vienna. But brie dates back even further than that. In the 15th century, Charles d'Orléans, father of Louis XII, used to order bries by the dozen to give to his friends as New Year presents.
There are many different varieties, but when you are choosing any of them look for a round cheese that bulges, rather than runs, when you press it. It should be pale yellow with a reddish crust streaked with white.

The Ile de France is also known for its rich soft creamy cheeses. If you want to sample something relatively local try:

Boursin: famous soft cheese flavoured with herbs and garlic with a high fat content. Also exported and made in Normandy.

Brie de Coulommiers: a rich sharp cheese, often used in cooking. Sometimes with added cream. Not the same as the commercially produced coulommiers.

Brie laitier: a commercially produced pasteurised cheese.

Brie de Meaux fermier: the King of Cheeses. Look for a white crust, slightly marked with red or brown. The inside is pale yellow and slightly firm.

A tempting display of cheeses, typical of any delicatessen

FOOD AND DRINK

Brie de Melun: reputed to be even older that the Meaux. Made from raw cow's milk and produced in small dairies in the traditional manner. A bit smellier than the Meaux and generally squatter and thicker.

Brie de Montereau: Also known as Ville St-Jacques. A bit like a camembert but with a fruitier flavour.

Chévru: an up-market cheese a bit like a Meaux. Made on a farm and also known as fougère or fougèru.

Coulommiers: a smaller version of the Meaux. Sold commercially when the straw it is supposed to mature on is often plastic. A creamy cheese with a white crust.

Délice de St-Cyr: a rich creamy cheese to eat with a fruity wine. Triple cream cheese with a mild flavour.

Explorateur: the commercial variety of a triple cream cheese.

Feuille de Dreux: when they made it at home it was wrapped in chestnut leaves. Low-fat cheese made from partially skimmed milk with a strong flavour.

Fontainebleau: fresh, rich, creamy dessert cheese made with whipped cream. Eaten

The food markets are always lively and are excellent places to buy all kinds of cheeses

with sugar, cold.
Ville St-Jacques: another name
for the brie de Montereau.

Wines

What to Look For
AC or AOC: *Appellation
contrôlée* on a label means you
should be getting a decent wine
with a guarantee of origin, of
production method and of grape
variety used.
The quantity produced is also
controlled. Although this is not
always enough to tell you if the
wine is particularly good. Good

*A quality wine is recognised by the
name of its château (estate)*

Bordeaux wines, for example, are
also recognised by the name of
the château they come from.
VDQS: *Vins Délimités de Qualité
Supérieure* denotes a wine
produced to encourage the
improvement of mediocre wines
(many of them from the south of
France).
Vins du pays: good value or
sometimes better, made from
specified variety of grape from
the area indicated on the bottle.
Vin de table: may be made from
a mixture of grape types or a
blend, not even necessarily from
France.

Wines to Take Home
You should know what you want
before you start shopping for
wine to take home – there is
more to a wine than just the label.
It is always worth looking for the
special offers in the
supermarkets such as Monoprix,
where even the ordinary prices

Wine With Your Cheese
There are no rules when it
comes to choosing a wine to
drink with your cheese. Any
strong cheese will completely
obscure the flavour of the wine
anyway. Choose a good quality
wine only if your cheese is mild
and in the best possible
condition. To be general and
safe, try a red Bordeaux for a
strong cheese, a white
Bordeaux or Burgundy for a
creamy one, or a glass of cold
champagne.

As a rough guide:
Blue veined cheeses (*bleu de
Bresse*) need a young red wine
like a Moulin à Vent, a sweet
white, or even port.
Creamy cheese (brie or
camembert) go with most
wines, especially if their flavour
is on the mild side.
Goat cheeses (*chèvre*) need a
white with a strong flavour like a
Sancerre or a sweet wine like a
Sauternes.

FOOD AND DRINK

are usually well below those of the wine merchants.

Well worth investing in are liqueurs like the blackcurrant-flavoured **cassis** to use with white wine to make Kir.

You can also buy unflavoured **eaux de vie** to preserve fruit, or flavoured varieties to drink as a liqueur, like pear or raspberry.

*The label on the bottle will tell you a certain amount about the quality of the wine – but the only way to discover its own particular flavour and aroma is to try a glassful
Below: an open-air wine-tasting at a château*

Grand Vin de Bordeaux

1985

SAUTERNES

Appellation Sauternes Contrôlée

Servir Frais

Product of France

75 cl

Mis en bouteille à Sainte-Eulalie (Gde) par ENGERBAUD
Négociant à Bordeaux 33000

ACCOMMODATION

There are hotels of every sort in Paris. Depending on your budget you will not be stuck for choice, though you may be for a vacancy if you arrive in the middle of a large trade fair or exhibition. You cannot go far wrong if you choose from the red *Michelin* guide (they publish a slim booklet solely on Paris). But pick your area carefully (see **The Different Areas** pages 11–20). You can get a free booklet listing a selection of Paris hotels from the tourist office who will also help you find a room.
The busiest times of year are June, September and October, and a useful leaflet, *Choose the best periods for your stay*, is available from the tourist office.

Eating in Hotels

Customary waking-up noises in Paris are the clatter of dustbin lids and the whine of street-cleaning trucks, church bells, shop shutters being rolled up and police car sirens. Pull open your own shutters and you may be able to smell newly baked croissants and strong coffee, although the aromas may not be coming from your own hotel. Although you can get breakfast in all hotels, in cheaper hotels it may be better to go down the road to a nearby bar rather than face slow service, stale buns, cartons of sterilised milk and undrinkable coffee.
Only the relatively expensive hotels have full restaurants. Unless your hotel is well known for its restaurant, it is better to eat out. See pages 65–74.

Bed and Breakfast

The tourist office issues a guide, *Résidences de Tourisme*, which lists star-rated apartments. But you can also rent an apartment or stay with a Parisian family through the organisation Chambres chez l'habitant et appartements équipés. Contact

Breakfast in elegant surroundings at the Hôtel de Crillon

ACCOMMODATION

The lavishly decorated Crillon hotel, an 18th-century palace at place de la Concorde

them at 73 rue Notre-Dame des Champs, 6e (tel: 43 25 43 97). Café-Couette is a network of families who wish to meet overseas guests and welcome them like friends into their own homes. They publish a list of host members in France (available for a fee through the tourist office).

Hotels
Expensive

The most exclusive and expensive hotels are in the 8e and the 1er *arrondissements*. One of these luxury hotels is the 18th-century **de Crillon** (tel: 44 71 15 00) a former palace on the place de la Concorde, with elegant yet intimate salons and sumptuous marble restaurant, Les Ambassadeurs. Others include the opulent **Plaza-Athénée** in among the *haute couture* salons of the avenue Montaigne, 8e (tel: 47 23 78 33); the **Ritz** in the place Vendôme, 1er, with its splendid Louis XV salons and rococo bedrooms (tel: 42 60 38 30). It has a splendid new health club, complete with all the most modern facilities and fads, including underwater music in the marble pool. The grand **Bristol** (tel: 42 66 91 45) in the rue du Faubourg-St-Honoré, 8e has Gobelin tapestries, old masters and a swimming pool;

Traditional elegance in the peaceful courtyard of the exclusive Lancaster hotel

and the small, refined and elegantly old fashioned **Lancaster** (tel: 43 59 90 43) with a pretty courtyard in the relatively quiet rue de Berri off the Champs-Elysées, 8e. Do not be afraid to enter the foyers of these luxury hotels, to sit down and take the weight off your feet. You are unlikely to be turned away, look as if you are a customer and enjoy the comings and goings of those who are. The Left Bank has fewer luxury hotels. One of them is the tiny **L'Hôtel Guy-Louis-Duboucheron** (tel: 43 25 27 22) at 13 rue des Beaux-Arts in St-Germain-des-Prés, 6e, where Oscar Wilde died. The decor is mildly eccentric and it has a popular tropical winter garden and piano bar. On the Left Bank, the 7e offers the **Pont Royal** (tel: 45 44 38 27) at 7 rue Montalembert. In the respectable part of the 9e, you will find the **Grand Hotel Inter Continental** at 2 rue Scribe (tel: 40 07 32 32) with its famous restaurant the Opéra-Café de la Paix, and the **Scribe** next door (tel: 44 71 24 24). Further out in the 11e arrondissement there is the **Holiday Inn** (tel: 43 55 44 34) in the place de la République. Business people tend to stay at

ACCOMMODATION

the **Méridien Montparnasse** (tel: 44 36 44 36) or the **Pullman Saint-Jacques** (tel: 40 78 79 80) in the 14e.

Alternatively, the **Hilton** (tel: 42 73 92 00), the **Sofitel** (tel: 40 60 30 30) with its indoor pool, or the ultra modern **Nikko de Paris** (tel: 40 58 20 00) are in the 15e.

The **Cidotel Park Avenue Central Park** (tel: 45 53 44 60) and the elegant Louis XVI-style **Raphaël** (tel: 44 28 00 28) near the Arc de Triomphe, are in the fashionable residential 16e. In the 17e you will find the huge, modern 1,000-roomed **Concorde Lafayette** (tel: 40 68 50 68), which has splendid views from the bar on the 34th floor and the even bigger, over-1,000-roomed **Méridien Paris Etoile** (tel: 40 68 34 34) which is well known for its jazz.

Reasonable

There are, of course, plenty of other, less expensive possibilities. Hundreds of three-star hotels offer varying degrees of service and comfort. To pick out just a few of the more central hotels:

On the Left Bank you could not choose a better location than the rue Jacob in St-Germain-des-Prés, 6e. There are several excellent hotels in this street including number 44 where Hemingway lived, now the **Angleterre** (tel: 42 60 34 72) with its conservatory-style garden; the **Danube St Germain** (tel: 42 60 94 07); and the quiet **des Marronniers** (tel: 43 25 30 60), with antiques and old wooden beams.

On the Ile St Louis, 4e, the sister hotels **des Deux Iles** (tel: 43 26

The 400-year-old Henri IV hotel, one of the cheapest in the capital, in the place Dauphine on the Ile de Cité

13 35) and **Lutèce** (tel: 43 26 23 52) are also quiet retreats

In the ler the Regency style **des Tuileries** (tel: 42 61 04 17) is in the rue Saint-Hyacinthe near the place Vendôme and in the same area Paris's oldest hotel the **Molière** (tel: 42 96 22 01), once used as a theatre, is in the rue Molière.

In the 8e the **Bradford** (tel: 45 63 20 20) in rue St-Philippe-du-Roule is one of the most reasonably priced hotels near the Champs-Elysées.

Also very central is the **Résidence la Concorde** (tel: 42 60 38 89) in the rue Cambon, ler, almost opposite the Tuileries, a good example of an Abotel Tradotel, a group of some 120 hotels situated throughout France in traditional buildings of character, which have been completely modernised to three-star standards (tel: 47 27 15 15).

Cheap

At the lower end of the market there are plenty of decent two-star hotels and surprisingly acceptable one-stars. You may not get a lounge area, private bathroom, bar or restaurant and it could be a steep hike up to the fifth floor without a lift. While some cheaper hotels are little gems, tucked away in quiet side streets (or at least with rooms overlooking quiet courtyards), others are drab, noisy and grimy. You may be kept awake by noisy plumbing, creaking beds from the room next door, flickering neons or traffic. Although there are plenty of cheap hotels in desirable areas, like the 6e, 5e, or 4e, be careful of those around the Gare du Nord (10e) or Pigalle (9e). As

converted out of 17th-century houses. Equally historic is the **Bretonnerie** (tel: 48 87 77 63) in rue Ste-Croix-de-la-Bretonnerie across the Seine in the Marais (in the street where gay Paris tends to congregate).

ACCOMMODATION

well as being noisy you may also find that your hotel is being used for some less desirable activities and women who do not want to be pestered may prefer to choose a more salubrious area.

The following are cheap, comfortable and central:

On the Left Bank in the 6e, the **Welcome** (tel: 46 34 24 80) in the rue de Seine right on top of the food market, the 17th-century **Hôtel du Globe** (tel: 43 26 35 50) in the rue des Quatre-Vents with its antiques and old beams and the **Récamier** (tel: 43 26 04 89) in the place St-Sulpice, quiet but very central, opposite the church of St-Sulpice.

In the 5e there is the 17th-century **Esmeralda** (tel: 43 54 19 20), on six floors with no lift, old-fashioned but with a lot of character, at 4 rue St-Julien-le-Pauvre near Notre-Dame. Or the **Grands Écoles** (tel: 43 26 79 23) at 75 rue du Cardinal-Lemoine, not grand at all but a comfortable country house with garden.

Across the Seine, if you want to be near the Louvre on the Right Bank you could try the modern **Ducs de Bourgogne** (tel: 42 33 95 64) at 19 rue du Pont-Neuf, 1er, or the **Hotel Family** (tel: 42 61 54 84) at 35 rue Cambon, 1er. On the Ile de la Cité the **Henry IV** (tel: 43 54 44 53) in a 400-year-old building overlooks the quiet place Dauphine. It is fairly basic, but very cheap.

In the Marais you will find relative peace in the **Places des Vosges** (tel: 42 72 60 46) at 12 rue Birague, 4e, and at the **Vieux Marais** (tel: 42 78 47 22) at 8 rue du Platre, 4e.

Youth Hostels

The Accueil des Jeunes en France (AJF) have 8,000 beds all year round and 11,000 available in the summer, when they use the Cité Universitaire. The head office is at 12 rue des Barres, 4e (tel: 42 72 72 09), or you can visit them at the Gare du Nord arrival hall (March to November); opposite the Pompidou Centre at 119 rue St-Martin, 4e (open all year); at the Hôtel-de-Ville at 16 rue du Pont-Louis-Philippe 4e (June to September); or in the 5e in the Latin Quarter at 139 boulevard St-Michel (March to October).

The offices also offer an information service, meal vouchers, student restaurants and reduced cost train and coach tickets. In summer the office at the Gare du Nord is open seven days a week from 08.00 to 22.00. The other offices (except the one opposite the Pompidou Centre which is open on Saturday) are only open from Monday to Friday.

With international Youth Hostel Association membership you can reserve a place at:

Auberge de Jeunesse Jules Ferry, 8 boulevard Jules Ferry, Paris 75011 (tel: 43 57 55 60); or Auberge de Jeunesse D'Artagnan, 80 rue Vitruve, Paris 75020 (tel: 43 61 08 75).

Accueil de France, run by the tourist board (office at the top of the Champs-Elysées open every day, offices at main stations closed Sundays, and at the Eiffel Tower daily summer only) also have cheap accommodation on their books.

PARIS BY NIGHT

There are endless night-time
possibilities in Paris, from sleazy
jazz clubs to glamorous
cabarets. There is no one
specific area for nightlife,
although different activities tend
to concentrate themselves into
one area. If you want to head for
a concentration of lively streets
and after-dark activities try:

The Left Bank

The streets around St-Germain-
des-Prés (6e) are full of late night
bars, cafés and jazz clubs. The
rue de la Huchette has many
ethnic restaurants and a good
jazz club, and the boulevard
Saint-Michel is always packed
until the small hours. The

See the lights by bâteau mouche

boulevard du Montparnasse and
the rue de la Gaîté in the 14e
offer discos, sex shows and
neons although on a much
smaller scale than, for example,
Pigalle.

The Right Bank

The red light district is Pigalle
(9e and 18e) around the
boulevard de Clichy (see **Sex
Shows**, below). The streets
around the Forum des Halles,
going towards Châtelet are lively
late at night. The partly
pedestrian-only rue des
Lombards is full of jazz clubs; the
neons and sex shows are in the
rue St-Denis. In the Marais (4e),

The can-can girls at the Moulin Rouge – familiar to many from Toulouse-Lautrec's posters – are still kicking, 100 years on

door or box office although, as in all major cities, popular venues and well known artists get booked up very quickly so it is as well to try and buy them in advance. The FNAC bookshops sell tickets for concerts, pop and classical. Branches in the Forum des Halles (2nd level) and on the Left Bank at 136 rue de Rennes, 6e.

Other ticket agencies are listed in the **Directory**. They all charge a booking fee.

What's On

To find out what's on get the weekly *l'Officiel des Spectacles* (Wednesdays, in French); *Pariscope*; the free *Paris Sélection* monthly magazine published by the tourist board; or the English language *Passion* magazine (published every two months by London's *Time Out* and similar in style but with more articles and fewer listings).

Where to Go

Cabaret

Can-can girls, performing seals, erupting volcanoes, bare bosoms and champagne are what the Paris cabarets are all about. They are pretty tame and although the shows pander to the male contingent of the audience, most men take their wives or at least their girlfriends. You will not see many Francophiles in the audience and the dancing girls will probably not be from Paris at all – their legs are not long enough – but it is all good fun and most of the shows are pretty spectacular.

Before the show there is often a dinner dance which adds another couple of hundred francs

you will find discreet clubs and discos in the rue Vieille du Temple, and a concentration of gay bars in the rue Ste-Croix-de-la-Bretonnerie.

The Bastille (11e) has a few strip clubs and sleazy dives, plus trendy bars and nightclubs with live music plus an old-time musical hall, all concentrated in a low-key triangle around the rue de Charonne, rue de Lappe and rue de la Roquette.

In all these areas there is a danger of petty theft. Watch your bag and be polite if you do not want trouble.

Tickets

You can get tickets for most clubs, concerts and shows at the to the bill. You can buy a ticket just for the 'spectacle', or 'la revue' as they call it, which usually includes at least one drink. Most cabarets have two or three shows a night, some starting after midnight.

Tickets at the door are much less than the 'all-in' evening excursions sold by tour operators, even if they do include half a bottle of champagne and a coach back to your hotel. You can also buy them through agencies.

There are over 40 cabaret venues in Paris, the following among the better known:

Crazy Horse Saloon 12 avenue George V, 8e (tel: 47 23 32 32) Theatrical extravaganza in which the evening is devoted to the admiration of the female form starring, among others, Betty Buttocks.

Folies Bergère 32 rue Richer, 9e (tel: 42 46 77 11) Famous since the 1860s for its half-naked girls, frilly costumes and coloured feathers, the Folies Bergère recently broke away from tradition to offer its audience a fast-moving, sparkling and typically French variety show with an emphasis on singing, sumptuous decors and good humour.

Lido 116 bis avenue des Champs-Elysées, 8e (tel: 45 63 11 61) On the Champs-Elysées. Expensive but worth the money for a show that costs several million pounds to put on. The spectacular effects and light show include anything from performing elephants to erupting volcanoes and skaters. The 60 Bluebell girls are

choreographed by a computer. Do not expect to be able to get a taxi when you get out unless you have booked one in advance. **Moulin Rouge** 83 boulevard de Clichy, 18e (tel: 46 06 00 19) Immortalised by Toulouse Lautrec, one of Paris's oldest cabarets, celebrated 100 years of the can-can in 1989, slap in the middle of the red-light district.

Cinema
English-language films with French sub-titles are shown at cinemas along the Champs-Elysées. Original language films are also shown at cinemas in the Latin Quarter (often oldies) and at the **Cinémathèque Française** at the Palais de Tokyo and the Palais de Chaillot.

If you want to be sure about the original language look for the initials VO. Films that have been dubbed into French will say VF. Paris is packed with cinemas. Several have more than one screen under the same roof – there are six in the **Gaumont Les Halles**, 1 rue Pierre Lescot, Porte Rombuteau. **Le Grand** (1 boulevard Poissonnière, 2e) has seven. In **La Pagode** (57 bis rue de Babylone, 7e) is a stunning Far Eastern pavilion decorated with dragons and elephants. If you do not fancy the film you can always drop in for a cup of tea. Although the commentary is in French and there are no sub-titles, if you want a cinerama-like experience it is worth going to **La Géode** at La Villette (19e), the new 180-degree screen in a mirrored dome, with six-track stereo that wraps itself around your lateral vision. Worth the experience especially if you

have children with you (open
10.00 to 21.00, closed Mondays).
Do not forget to tip the
usherettes. Monday nights are
cheaper. Children, students and
senior citizens get a reduction on
all other days except Fridays and
weekends.

Classical Concerts

Free (*libre*) concerts are held in
churches (*église*) all over Paris.
Look in one of the weekly
magazines for what's on while
you are there.

The National Orchestra of France
also gives free concerts at
Maison de Radio France, 116
avenue du Président-Kennedy,
16e. (tel: 42 30 23 08).

Other concert venues include:

● L'Auditorium (Théâtre
Musical de Paris, Forum des
Halles, Porte Sainte-Eustache,
1er (tel: 42 33 00 00)

● Epicerie-Beaubourg, 12 rue du
Renard, 4e (tel: 42 72 23 41)

● Salle Cortot, 78 rue Cardinet,
17e (tel: 47 63 80 16)

● Salle Gaveau, 45 rue de la
Boétie, 8e (tel: 49 53 05 07)

● Salle Pleyel, 252 rue du

Faubourg St-Honoré, 8e (tel: 45
61 06 30)

● Théâtre des Champs-Elysées,
15 avenue Montaigne, 8e (tel: 47
20 36 37)

● Théâtre Musical de Paris, 1
place du Châtelet, 1er (tel: 40 28
28 40)

Dance

The Opéra de Paris-Garnier at 8
rue Scribe, place de l'Opéra, 9e
(tel: 47 42 53 71) is the home of
the French classical ballet in
Paris. The baroque theatre holds
2,000 people who sit in
splendour under the magnificent
ceiling by Chagall. Even if you
cannot afford a ticket you can still
go in.

Contemporary dance venues are
mostly in the 11e around the
Bastille including:

● Théâtre de la Bastille (also
fringe drama), 76 rue de la
Roquette, 11e (tel: 43 57 42
14)

● Ménagerie de Verre, 12 rue
Lechevin (tel: 43 38 33 44)

*Paris by night – many of the
monuments and some of the
bridges over the Seine are floodlit*

● The Café de la Danse, 5 passage Louis-Philippe (tel: 43 57 05 35)

● Studio La Forge, 18 rue de la Forge Royale (tel: 43 71 71 89) Touring companies perform and occasional dance programmes are held at:

● The American Centre, 261 boulevard Raspail, 14e (tel: 43 21 42 20)

● The Casino de Paris, 16 rue de Clichy, 9e (tel: 48 74 15 80)

● Théâtre de Paris, 15 rue Blanche, 9e (tel: 48 78 52 22)

● The vast Palais des Sports, Porte de Versailles, 15e (tel: 48 28 40 90)

Jazz

There are numerous bars in Paris offering live jazz, from the sleazy, smoky basements in the Latin Quarter and around Les Halles to big American bands who perform in the unlikely setting of the Méridien hotel in the 17e and in the huge warehouse Le Dunois out in the 13e.

Jazz is undergoing something of a revival in Paris. You will find many of the clubs in St-Germain-des-Prés on the Left Bank, and along the partly pedestrian-only rue des Lombards, (1er, 4e) near Châtelet on the Right.

Most jazz clubs do not get going until midnight or so and stay open until three or four in the morning. Many also serve food. Turn up fairly early if you want a seat, otherwise be prepared to stand. You usually have to pay an amount at the door, depending on the calibre of the musicians, and for drinks on top of that, though some charge an amount for the first drink that takes care

of the entrance fee.

There are too many jazz venues to cover them all but among the most popular are:

Le Sunset (one of many in the rue des Lombards), attracts top musicians, small, lively and decorated like a Métro station, open every night from 22.30; 60 rue des Lombards, 1er.

Le Baiser Salé at number 58 offers contemporary jazz bands as well as live soul and African music upstairs. From 22.30. Or try the **Duc des Lombards** at number 42, a small, sophisticated bar with jazz piano on Friday and Saturday nights as well as noisy Afro-American Parisian residents.

Le Petit Opportun (15 rue des Lavendières-Sainte-Opportune, 1er), in a basement, stays open until 03.00 if you have the energy. If you cannot get a seat they play tapes in the bar upstairs. In the 10e, near St-Lazare, real jazz enthusiasts head for the large **New Morning** (7–9 rue des Petites-Ecuries 10e, near Brasserie Flo).

It is a bit impersonal compared to some of the dingy basements, and holds 400 people, but it attracts big names in jazz, as well as pop, salsa, African and Brazilian bands. Concerts usually start at 21.30.

On the Left Bank, the intimate **Le Bilboquet** (13 rue St-Benoît, 6e) offers jazz bands of various nationalities who perform in a long, narrow art-nouveau railway carriage of a room, on the ground floor of the hotel, from 22.30. Near by, **Le Village** (7 rue Gozlin, 6e) on the other side of the boulevard St-Germain is where to spot new talent, and they also serve food.

In the neighbouring 5e, the **Caveau de la Huchette** (5 rue de la Huchette) is one of the last true *caves*, a smoky, small, stone vaulted basement, with a dance floor, open from 21.30 to 02.30 (03.00 on Fridays) and until 04.00 on Saturdays.

Over in Montparnasse in the 14e, **Le Petit Journal Montparnasse** (13 rue du Commandant-René-Mouchotte) has nightly changing bands, mostly French and well known names. You can eat and it is open from 21.00 to 02.00. Popular, but a bit far out in the 13e, is **Le Dunois** (28 rue Dunois near the Métro Chevaleret), a vast warehouse where improvised jazz comes into its own with visiting big bands. And, in the 17e, the **Méridian Jazz Trad** in the Méridian Hotel (81 boulevard Gouvion-Saint-Cyr) offers good jazz (Monday to Saturday, 22.00 to 02.00) in an up-market setting (also Sunday lunchtime).

Live Music

Also see **Jazz** (above) and **Nightclubs/Discos** (below). Bands play at a number of venues, some of which are huge concert halls, others are clubs where you can drink and dance. You can hear rock, salsa, African, Caribbean and plenty of other nationalities.

Rock Band Venues

Rock bands play to relatively small audiences at the **Forum des Halles**; **Olympia** (28 boulevard des Capucines, 9e) in the old music hall and at **Rock 'n' Roll Circus**, (6 rue Caumartin, 9e).

The large venues include:

The **Palais des Congrès** Porte Maillot, 17e, where famous international bands perform in an auditorium that seats 3,700; the modern **Palais Omnisports de Bercy** (8 boulevard de Bercy, 12e) which can seat 17,000 and the **Palais des Sports** at the Porte de Versailles, 15e, another enormous venue. **Le Zénith** in the Parc de La Villette (211 boulevard Jean-Jaurès, 19e) is an inflatable stadium with seating for 6,500.

Nightclubs/Discos

Nightclubs with live bands and discos go in and out of fashion. Entry is often at the discretion of the person on the door. In some it pays off to look scruffy, at others you will not be allowed in unless you are done up to the nines or wearing suitably trendy garb. Nothing much happens this side of midnight. Your concierge (if you are staying somewhere that has one) will help with venues and may swing you admittance for a small fee. Clubs that seem to be fairly consistently popular or at least worth going to for the decor and atmosphere include:

Les Bains in a former Turkish bath house (7 rue du Bourg-L'Abbé, 3e). Expensive. Sometimes live rock, otherwise people-watching is fun enough. Clubby atmosphere. Upstairs restaurant.

The Rose Bon Bon (34 rue de la Roquette, 11e), near the Bastille or **Le Gibus** (18 rue du Faubourg-du-Temple, 11e). Both with live rock bands.

Le Balajo is in an old fashioned 40s-style music hall (9 rue de Lappe, 11e). Open Thursday,

Friday, Saturday and Monday from 22.00 to 04.30. Revolving glittery globe above the dance-floor, with a band on a sequinned balcony. Saturday afternoon for old-time dancing. Evenings for up-to-the-minute stuff. **Le Tango** (13 rue au Maire, 3e) is another venue for real dancing whether it is reggae or a rhumba. Open Wednesday to Saturday.
Le Palace (3 Cité Bergère, 9e) attracts a mixed crowd of all ages, a big popular disco still going strong after ten years or so. Various theme nights. If you eat first in the restaurant you get free entrance. Dress up. Open nightly.
La Locomotive (90 boulevard de Clichy, 18e) is on three floors, much of it under the Moulin Rouge. Different levels and dance floors. Trendy crowd.
Club O'Valère (40 rue du Colisée, 8e) is open until dawn for older sophisticated Parisians who have moved on from **Régine's** (49 rue de Ponthieu, 8e) piano bar, dance floor and restaurant. Expensive and can be difficult to get in.
L'Atmosphère (45 rue François ler, 8e), is just as sophisticated, but you may be lucky and be allowed in.

Opera
The Paris Opéra season is from the end of September to mid-July. For tickets apply to: L'Opéra de Paris Bastille, 2 bis place de la Bastille, 12e (tel: 44 73 13 00). This is the new home of the Opéra de Paris. The Palais Garnier (the former State Opera House) in the place de l'Opéra (near Galeries Lafayette) is now solely the home

The Lido on the Champs Elysées has the most extravagant floor show

of the French Ballet (see **Dance**). Opera is also performed at the Epicerie Beaubourg (see **Classical Concerts**) and at the Opéra-Comique at the Salle Favart, 5 rue Favart, 2e (tel: 42 96 06 11). Other venues include the Théâtre du Châtelet, 1 place du Châtelet, ler (tel: 40 28 28 40) and Théâtre du Lierre, 22 rue du Chevaleret, 13e (tel: 45 86 55 83).

Prostitutes
Prostitution is not illegal but soliciting is. The main areas are around Pigalle (9e and 18e), the rue St-Denis near the Forum des Halles, around the Opéra, behind the Madeleine in rue de Sèze, in the rue Daunou in the 2e, the rue de la Gaîté near Montparnasse in the 14e and in the avenue Foch in the 16e.

Pigalle – the seedy side of Paris

Sex Shows – Pigalle

Paris has its share of sleazy strip clubs, tattoo parlours, and live, or 'life' as they call them, sex shows. Many of them are private. Pigalle is where most of them are, in and around the boulevard Clichy, in the 9e *arrondissement* and just over the border into the 18e, which, with its narrow streets and dead-end alleyways, is even less salubrious. It is not all nightclubs – there are plenty of boutiques (with names like Derrière les Fagots) and hotels. In case you are offered a hotel in this area, the streets to avoid are those leading south off the boulevard Clichy, the rue Frochot, rue Henri-Monnier, rue Lafferière, rue Notre-Dame de Lorette, rue Chaptal and rue Blanche. It is not unheard of for tour operators 'innocently' to offer hotels in Pigalle, eulogising their proximity to the Moulin Rouge and Montmartre and for visitors to be shocked and angry to discover their proximity to the seedier side of Paris. Be warned and check out the address before you accept the booking.

Business in Pigalle apparently is not booming. The locals blame it on AIDS frightening off the tourists and the TGV high speed train which denies errant businessmen the old excuse to spend a night in the city and whisks them home to the suburbs in time for cocoa.

Other areas: Less sordid, with a handful of sex shows and plenty of neons, is the rue St-Denis near the forum des Halles, some of the streets around the Bastille (11e) and the rue de la Gaîté near Montparnasse (14e). The sex shows are still on offer but alongside other possibilities from art galleries to jazz clubs.

THE WEATHER

Winters in Paris are rather colder than in Britain; winds can be biting, and the quais along the Seine and the spacious boulevards and squares that make sightseeing such a pleasure afford little protection, so take warm clothing. In summer Paris tends to a more settled continental climate. Humidity and sun can be oppressive if you are doing a lot of sightseeing – a boat trip on the

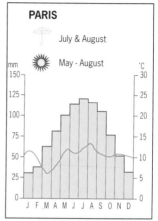

Left: painters in Montmartre

river can be a refreshing remedy. If you have access to a television, the weather forecast symbols (*météo*) are universal, even if you cannot understand French.

WHEN TO GO

Major trade fairs, fashion shows and art exhibitions govern how full or empty Paris is at any one time. The Office du Tourisme advise avoiding: mid-January, early February, first half of March, end of April, second half of May, June, September, October and mid-November when it can be difficult to find a hotel room (also see **Accommodation**, page 79). Other than that, the quietest time is generally March to May and November. Autumn can be pretty wet and New Year chilly and windy.

If you're planning to shop, a good time to visit is after Christmas for the January sales. If the purpose of your visit is to sample the restaurants don't forget to book well ahead and avoid July and August when many of the best restaurants close for their annual holidays. If you're planning a long weekend, include Friday rather than Monday when many galleries and museums are shut.

EVENTS

The French Government Tourist Office produce a free leaflet *Saisons de Paris* listing major events and exhibitions.

January
Fashion collections

February
Fashion collections

March
Agricultural Show
World Tourist and Travel Show

April
Paris Fair

EVENTS

The Paris Marathon, in April or May

May
French Tennis Championship
(until early June)
Paris Festival (until end of June)

June
Annual Flower Show – Bois de
Vincennes
Paris Air Show, Le Bourget
(every two years)
Paris Villages Festival

July
Bastille Day (14th). Fireworks
and military display, marking the
anniversary of the French
Revolution
Finish of the Tour de France (last
Sunday, Champs-Elysées)
Fashion collections
Festival Estival (concerts until
mid-September)

August
Parisians go on holiday

September
Autumn Festival (music, theatre,
dance – mid-September to the
end of December)

October
International Contemporary Arts
Exhibition, Grand Palais

November
Armistice Day (11th). Military
displays at the Arc de Triomphe

December
Antiques Fair, Espace Austerlitz
International Boat Show

HOW TO BE A LOCAL

In a world where life is becoming increasingly humdrum and cosmopolitan, national traits and characteristics are under serious threat. Paris has been no less subject to this trend than anywhere else, so being a local is not the specialised art it once was; but its attractions and its population remain unique. A lot of the chic has gone, especially among the younger generation, though older Parisians are still often fairly unmistakable, either through their easy elegance or through essential accoutrements like berets.

See them at their best in the street markets, where they banter and haggle.

Popular pastimes include short strolls through the parks, by the river and along the boulevards, the last being punctuated by stops at pavement bars and cafés. These have traditionally been favourite spots to see and be seen, particularly those on the Champs-Elysées and the boulevard St-Germain. But these places are usually quite expensive, and the older locals will tell you that there's much less to see, fewer fashions to turn heads, less chic to admire, less 'proper' Paris. But style there still is, and correct service from smartly attired staff is something that Parisians still demand and still generally get. Parisians are effusive in their greeting and always seem to find time for conversation. Topics are much the same as anywhere else, with the addition of an obsession with their health.

In brief, to be a local, you need to be enthusiastic and outgoing, something which should come fairly naturally as soon as Paris has begun to cast its spell.

Feeding the pigeons in the park, a pastime for young and old

Au Restaurant

Parisians rich and poor have always liked their food and know exactly what they want. Even in Paris the restaurant scene is inevitably slipping into fast gear. But right-minded locals ensure the continued existence of back-street bistros, where good simple French food is still available. In the more up-market establishments, a detailed knowledge of and close interest in the menu marks out Parisians. Sunday lunchtime often brings three generations together *en famille* and it is fascinating to see that even the very young and the very old will debate long about what to order.

CHILDREN

Paris does not cater particularly
well for young children although
older ones will enjoy the main
sites and under 18's get in free to
national museums. There are no
reductions on the Métro or buses
although under-threes are free.
Few restaurants have highchairs,
though many will serve small
portions if you ask them, but
there are so many fast-food
restaurants that finding cheap
snacks is easy. If you are taking a
baby you will have no problems
buying disposable nappies or
jars of babyfood and you can
hire a babysitter if you want a
night out without them. It does
not take long for all children to
discover that Paris is different
and for school-age children to try
out their French.

Children of all ages will enjoy:
riding up the escalator outside
Beaubourg and the free street
shows in the piazza outside;
taking the lift (or even the steps)
up the Eiffel Tower; climbing to
the top of Notre-Dame Cathedral
or the Arc de Triomphe and
riding in a *bateau mouche* along
the Seine. Remember that as well
as under 18s getting into national
museums free, on Sundays some
museums are free to everyone.
There are a number of
playgrounds in the main parks,
many with puppet shows (see
below), although unfortunately
you are not allowed to let
children run on the grass.

The French are, of course,
obsessed with dressing their
little darlings *á la mode*. There
are some superb shops for
children's clothes, including a
Baby Dior, Kenzo for kids, and

Parisian children dress à la mode.
*Kenzo's boutique for children is in
the place des Victoires*

lovely boutiques in the rue Jacob
(6e). The department stores,
especially Monoprix and Prisunic
are cheaper, though not that
cheap as in France there is tax
on children's clothes of 18.6 per
cent.

Babies

You can rent a pushchair (or a
cot or babysitter) from Maman
Poule (tel: 47 48 01 01; 24hrs).
For babysitting only try Kid's
Service (tel: 47 66 00 52); or
ABABA La Maman en Plus (tel: 43
22 22 11; closed Sundays). You
can buy familiar brands of
babyfood and babymilk and
disposable nappies (*couches à
jeter*) in supermarkets and
pharmacies.

Places to Visit

Most of the places listed below

have also been covered in other parts of this guide, so refer to the **Index**. Check in *Pariscope*, *Paris Sélection* or *l'Officiel des Spectacles* for the opening hours and times of special shows.

AQUABOULEVARD, 15e

A large park with an artificial lake where you can swim and sail boats, near the Porte de Sèvres. *Open*: 09.00 (08.00 Friday and Saturday) to 23.00 (24.00 Saturday and Sunday). *Métro*: Balard

...there's plenty in the streets and squares of Paris to tempt the young photographer

BEAUBOURG/GEORGES POMPIDOU CENTRE, 4e

Rues Rambuteau, Saint-Martin and Beaubourg

Make a beeline for Beaubourg even if you do not want to take the children into one of the changing exhibitions or the National Museum of Modern Art. On Wednesdays and Saturdays they run children's workshops with English-speaking playleaders.

There is also a children's library, open in the afternoons from 13.00 to 19.00 with an English section for 6–12's. The square outside is a free entertainment zone. There may be jugglers,

CHILDREN

musicians, artists, portrait painters, or clowns to keep them occupied.

The ride up the outside of the Pompidou Centre, on the glassed-in escalator, is free and fun with good views.

See also page 23.

CITÉ DES SCIENCES ET DE L'INDUSTRIE, La Villette, 19e

30 avenue Corentin Cariou

Vast hands-on museum on the site of the city abattoir, with computers, robots, machinery to work and buttons to press in an area several times the size of Beaubourg. There is a special area for children, with separate sections for ages three to six, and five to twelve.

Unfortunately few of the instructions are in English except on a few computers, but headsets with a commentary are available in English. On the premiss that most children do not read instructions anyway, there is enough for them to work out for themselves to make it worth a visit. There is a dragon slide in the park behind the Cité and a huge mirrored dome, La Géode, shows 180-degree projection films (in French). One fee to get into the museum but extra charges for La Géode and the planetarium.

See also pages 24-5.

EURO DISNEY RESORT

Marne-la-Vallée

Situated nearly 20 miles (32km) east of Paris, the European link in the Disney chain opened in 1992. The weather may be less predictable than its US counterparts, but the appeal of the five themed areas: Main

Children as well as adults will enjoy the Musée d'Orsay's Impressionist paintings

Street, Frontierland, Adventureland, Fantasyland and Discoveryland, is undiminished. For easy access, you can stay in one of six hotels, or the campsite.

Open: 09.00–10.00 to 18.00–24.00, depending on the season. (to check, tel: 49 41 49 10)

RER: Line A, Chessy-Marne-la-Vallée

(see also *Euro Disney Resort* guide in the *Essential* series)

identification; 686 feet (209m) high. There is an open-air terrace on the 59th floor. See also page 35.

MUSÉE D'ORSAY, 7e
1 rue de Bellechase
Magnificent art collection in the former railway station. Works by the Impressionist painters Renoir, Monet and Degas on the top floor. A good introduction to some of the world's most famous paintings. Pleasant views across the Seine to the Right Bank from the terrace by the café on the top floor. Visit the stunningly palatial restaurant on the first floor. See also page 22.

MUSÉE DES ARTS AFRICAINS ET OCÉANIENS, 12e
293 avenue Daumesnil
At the entrance of the Bois de Vincennes. It has a tropical aquarium as well as displays of the arts and crafts of Africa and Oceania and you could combine it with the zoo.
Métro: Porte Dorée
Open: 10.00 to 12.00 and 13.30 to 17.30 (weekends 12.30 to 18.00)
Closed: Tuesdays

LE PARC ASTERIX
A new leisure park with 100 attractions and six 'worlds' to explore; among these are the world of Astérix, Ancient Rome and the world of the imagination. Reached by shuttle service from Charles-de-Gaulle RER station. 24 miles (38km) from Paris, near Roissy/Charles-de-Gaulle Airport.
Open: April to October daily. Wednesdays and weekends in winter.

EIFFEL TOWER, (TOUR EIFFEL) 7e
Champs de Mars
You can get a lift up to the first, second and third stages. On the first floor there is an audio-visual of the history of the tower which was built in 1889 for the World Exhibition.
See also page 31.

TOUR MONTPARNASSE, 15e
33 avenue du Maine
Get the lift up to the 56th floor in 38 seconds, for great views of the capital with telescopes to help with

CHILDREN

PARC OCEANIQUE COUSTEAU, 1er
Forum des Halles
A great adventure for children. Journeying through space, plunging to Earth, into the sea, you explore the creatures of the deep from the safety of your vessel. Back on the surface climb inside a life-size model of a blue whale, or learn about marine life from hands-on video displays.
Open: 10.00 to 17.30 (16.00 Tuesday and Thursday)
Closed: Monday
Métro: Les Halles, *RER*: Châtelet-les-Halles

The pond in the Tuileries Gardens is the place for sailing boats

Boats
A boat ride along the Seine in a *bateau mouche* or *vedette* is well worth doing, just for the fun of it and also because most of the well known monuments can be seen along the banks. Boats are large, covered and there are English commentaries. They are run by different companies and leave from various points: Pont de l'Alma, Pont d'Iéna (opposite the Eiffel Tower), and Pont Neuf (near the Louvre).

101

Night-time excursions to see the illuminations are more expensive, as are boats with tea or dinner on board. (See also **Canals**, page 108.)
For barge rides along the canals to La Villette, see pages 25 and 26.

Parks and Playgrounds
The Jardin d'Acclimatation in the Bois de Boulogne, 16e is the best place to take young children but it is not cheap. Take the Métro to Les Sablons or to Porte Maillot (afternoons only). If your children want a ride on a little train, choose an afternoon on a Wednesday, weekend or school holiday. Plenty to do and go on (rides, bowling, mini-golf, miniature farm and paddle boats down the enchanted river). All the rides are priced individually. The Bois de Boulogne has mini-golf, boating and bowling and you can hire bikes to ride through the woods.

There are **children's playgrounds** in the Parc Monceau, 17e (*Métro*: Monceau), and the Parc Floral (route de la Pyramide in the Bois de Vincennes) has a children's theatre (Astral) as well as plenty of things for children to do especially on summer weekends (*Métro*: Château de Vincennes). The Jardin des Plantes, 5e (*Métro*: Gare d'Austerlitz) has a mini zoo, aquarium and a maze. The Jardin du Luxembourg, 6e has a playground, pony rides, toy boats and puppet theatre (*RER*: Luxembourg) and the Jardin des Tuileries, 1er (*Métro*: Tuileries, Concorde) has the famous octagonal pond on which Parisian children sail their boats.

There are also puppet shows in the Buttes-Chaumont park, on Wednesday and weekend afternoons at 15.15 and 16.15 in the Champ de Mars near the Eiffel Tower (*Métro*: Ecole-Militaire) and in the gardens at the Rond-Point north of the Champs-Elysées on Wednesdays and weekends at 15.00, 16.00 and 17.00.
If you are shopping in the Forum des Halles there is a children's garden with six different adventure worlds for seven to eleven-year-olds. In the park behind the Cité des Sciences et de l'Industrie there is a popular dragon slide. Also at La Villette there is a rock concert stadium, the Zénith and a 180-degree projection cinema screen La Géode, for films (only in French).

Skating
Roller-skating rink in the Parc Monceau, 17e and La Main Jaune at the Porte de Champerret, also in the 17e. There is an ice-skating rink in the Buttes-Chaumont, 30 rue Edouard Pailleron, 19e.
Métro: Bolivar.

Swimming
There is an outdoor pool, the Piscine Buttes-aux-Cailles at 5 place Paul-Verlaine, open in summer. Indoor and outdoor pools are listed in *Pariscope* under *Piscines* (swimming pools) and in the **Directory**, page 122.

Zoos
Nothing very exciting. There is a small zoo in the Jardin des Plantes, rue Cuvier, 5e and one in the Bois de Vincennes, avenue de St-Maurice, 12e.
Métro: Porte Dorée

TIGHT BUDGET

Paris need not be expensive. If you are on a budget there are plenty of cheap hotels and youth hostel accommodation. When you arrive look for the *hôtesses de Paris* at the railway station or at the airport. They will tell you which hotels have vacancies and generally point you in the right direction.

● Students can get reductions with an International Student Card. You must have proof that you are a full time student, a passport sized photo and 30F (currently). Go to the Council on International Education Exchange, 49 rue Pierre-Charron, 8e (tel: 45 63 19 87). With it you can get reductions to museums, films and on public transport.

● Don't buy a single ticket when travelling on the Métro or on buses. It is cheaper to buy a book (carnet) of tickets and invest in one of the cheap cards (see Tickets, page 114). The

Le Trumilou has been offering cheap meals for some 100 years

Carte Jeunes entitles under 26s to a 50 per cent reduction on trains in France between June and September, for example.

● Use your student card to get reductions on admission charges to museums or else join the queues on Sundays when some offer free admission. Alternatively, buy a Carte Musée et Monuments, offering unlimited visits to major museums and monuments for a single payment. Available from museums, larger Métro stations and tourist information offices.

● The cheapest restaurants are *Les Selfs* (self-service) in large department stores. Otherwise follow the local students on the Left Bank to cheap restaurants in the 5e *arrondissement*. There are specific student restaurants in the 5e and 6e or you can buy a take-away (Greek mostly) from the rue de la Huchette, 5e.

● Restaurants have their menus displayed outside – those with fixed prices for two or three courses are the best value.

● Drink house wine out of a jug or carafe.

● Avoid expensive bars in streets like the boulevard St-Germain and around Beaubourg. If you are thirsty head for a back street bar. Beer drinkers should ask for *un demi* (half) or *une pression* (draught) and remember that fizzy mineral water can be more expensive than wine!

● The cheapest places to buy clothes are Monoprix and Prisunic department stores, but the best 'designer' selection is at Galeries Lafayette. There are also cut price 'designer' shops where they sell off samples.

*The traffic speeding around the Arc de Triomphe is terrifying. Use the
pedestrian subway to get to the centre*

Contents

DIRECTORY

Arriving

Passports

British and other EC nationals and
citizens of the US, Canada and New
Zealand, need a valid passport
for a stay of up to three months.

Airports

Orly Airport (tel: 49 75 15 15)
Ten miles (16km) south of Paris.
To travel into Paris, the Orly Rail
(RER Line C) will take you to
Gare d'Austerlitz and stations on
the Left Bank. Trains leave every
15 minutes from 05.35 to 23.17,

and take about 35 minutes. Alternatively, Orlyval provides a connection with the RER (Line B) at Antony from 05.50 to 23.48 (every 4 to 7 minutes; every 15 minutes after 21.30). There are two bus possibilities. The cheaper Orly Bus goes direct to Denfert-Rochereau Métro near Montparnasse in the 14e on the Left Bank. It takes 25 minutes and buses leave every 12 minutes from 06.30 to 23.30. Or you can get the Air France bus to the place de Charles-de-Gaulle-Etoile. Buses leave every 20 minutes from 06.00 to 23.00 and the journey should take about 25 minutes.

Roissy/Charles-de-Gaulle Airport (tel: 48 62 22 80) Fourteen miles (23km) northeast of Paris.
To travel into Paris, the free airport shuttle bus will take you to the airport train station for

connections (RER Line B) into Paris. This is the quickest and most direct route. The journey takes 40 minutes to the Gare du Nord, from where you can change onto the Métro or get a taxi (there are sometimes queues). You can also continue by train to Châtalet-les-Halles which is nearer to the centre, and from where it is easier to get a taxi. Trains leave at 15-minute intervals between 04.59 and 23.59. The direct Air France bus (every 15 minutes) will drop you at Port Maillot (lower level of the Palais des Congrès) in the 17e, or at the place de Charles-de-Gaulle-Etoile (avenue Carnot) from where you can get a taxi or the Métro.
Buses run between 05.40 and 23.00. The Roissy Bus serves the

If you want to get anywhere in a hurry, go by Métro. If not, sit in a café until after the rush hour

Opéra district with departures every 15 minutes (journey time 45 minutes). Cheaper and slower (at least an hour) are the regular buses, number 350 to the Gare du Nord and the Gare de l'Est (every 20 minutes), and the 351 to the place de la Nation (every 30 minutes).

For both airports allow at least 50 minutes by taxi.

Camping
You can camp in the Bois de Boulogne all year round: Allée du Bord de l'Eau. Arrive early in summer as the site can be full by midday. An international camping carnet is necessary (tel: 45 24 30 00 for information).

Car Breakdown
If your car breaks down, the Paris 24-hour repair service can be contacted on tel: 47 07 99 99.

Car Hire
Agencies include:
Autorent tel: 45 54 22 45
Avis tel: 46 09 92 12
Budget France tel: 46 86 65 65
Europcar tel: 30 43 82 82
Hertz tel: 47 88 51 51
Inter Touring Service tel: 45 88 52 37 (including cars for the disabled)
Snac tel: 45 53 33 99
Thrifty tel: 05 16 02 75

Chauffeur-driven Cars
If you want a driver contact:
Executive Car Carey Limousine tel: 42 65 54 20
London Cab in Paris tel: 43 70 18 18
Murdoch Associés tel: 47 20 00 21 (UK tel: 0342 316428)
Bi-lingual drivers who will also act as personal assistants. All

cars have telephones.
Société des Chauffeurs tel: 46 34 77 07

Chemist (see Pharmacies)

Crime
Petty crime is high in Paris. Watch your bag on the Métro, in busy tourist areas like Beaubourg and the Champs-Elysées and in queues for museums. Be wary of seemingly innocent, scruffy-looking children – they will work the streets in gangs fleecing innocent tourists. Do not leave valuables visible in your car.

Customs Regulations
There are no limits on the importation of tax-paid goods purchased in an EC country. However, there are levels of alcohol and tobacco above which the importer (17 years and over) must be able to prove that these goods are for personal use only. For more detailed information contact the French Government Tourist Office.

Disabled Travellers
Useful guides are produced by Comité National Français de Liaison pour la Réadaptation des Handicapés, Point Handicap, 38 boulevard Raspail, 75007 Paris (tel: 45 48 98 90).

Domestic Travel
Driving in Paris
Parisians are notoriously reckless, fast drivers. You must, of course, drive on the right. The speed limit is 50kph (31mph) in built-up areas, 90kph (55mph) in

other areas, 110kph (68mph) on dual carriageways and non-toll motorways, and 130kph (80mph) on toll motorways (with 110kph/68mph limit on urban stretches). The speed limit on the Périphérique is 80kph (49mph). A minimum speed limit of 80kph (49mph) is in force on the outside lane of motorways during good daytime visibility. There are also wet weather limits of 80kph (49mph) outside built-up areas, 100kph (62mph) on dual carriageways and non-toll motorways, and 110kph (68mph) on toll motorways. In fog, with visibility down to 50 metres (55 yards) the limit is 50kph (31mph).

You must not exceed 90kph (55mph) if you have held a full driving licence for less than a year. The minimum driving age is 18. An international driving licence is not compulsory. A green card providing comprehensive insurance is not obligatory, but is strongly recommended.

As you approach the city do not on any account drive straight in. Take the Périphérique, the ring road, watching carefully for the nearest *porte* (exit) to your ultimate destination.

● **Parking**

If you are driving to Paris the best idea is to leave your car in one of the long-term car parks outside the Périphérique. There are also car parks in the city but they are more expensive. You cannot leave a vehicle for more than 24 consecutive hours in the same place in Paris and parking is prohibited on many streets in the centre.

Do not assume that because you bear foreign number plates you will be immune from the clamp, the tow-away truck or the wrath of the *pervenches* (blue-uniformed traffic wardens). If you are unfortunate enough to be clamped or your car is removed to the *fourrière* (police pound), ask the nearest *policier* or Commissariat de Police how to get it out. In the centre there are parking meters, or machines dispensing tickets on street corners. Street parking prohibitions are indicated by yellow markings on the kerb, or by street signs. Unfamiliar road signs may include those stating that parking is allowed on only one side of a street or that the gutters are due for a night clean. As for parking itself, nowhere in the world makes better use of the bumper.

Parisians squeeze themselves into the tiniest parking places, simply by shoving the car in front and behind out of the way. Should you be unfortunate enough to be one of them, you will find it impossible to get out of your well earned space. Paris is a relatively small city and the Métro is quick and convenient to use. Traffic is often very heavy indeed. A car is not really necessary.

● **Fuel**

In the UK the motorist uses a fuel according to star-ratings: 2-star 90 octane, 3-star 93 octane, 4-star 97 octane, unleaded 95 octane. In France petrol is graded as *Normale* or *Super* and visiting motorists should be careful to use a grade in the recommended range as many modern engines designed to run

Lunch on board a **bâteau mouche,** *but* **be warned** *– it will be very expensive*

on 4-star petrol are critical on carburation and ignition settings. Additionally, as unleaded petrol is also being sold, it is important to purchase the correct petrol. If a car designed to run on leaded petrol is filled with unleaded petrol it will do no immediate harm, provided it is the correct octane rating and the next fill is of leaded petrol.
Petrol (leaded): *Essence normale* (90 octane) and *essence super* (98 octane)
Petrol (unleaded): *Essence sans plomb* (95 octane) and *essence super sans plomb* (98 octane)
Diesel: *Gasoil* or *Gazolle*
To ask for a full tank, say, *faites-le-plein, s'il vous plaît.*

● **Registration Document**
You must carry the original vehicle registration document with you. If the vehicle is not registered in your name, you should have a letter from the owner authorising you to use it. If you are using a UK registered hired or leased vehicle, the registration document will not be available and a Hired/Leased Vehicle Certificate (VE103A), which may be purchased from the AA, should be used in its place.

● **Road Signs**
Most road signs are internationally agreed and the majority will be familiar to motorists.
Watch for road markings – do not cross a solid white or yellow line marked on the road centre.

● **Rules of the Road**
In France, drive on the right and overtake on the left. In addition, you must give way to traffic approaching from the right (*priorité à droite*) in built-up areas. Outside built-up areas, all traffic on main roads has

the right of way (*passage protégé*).

● **Seat Belts**

If your car is fitted with seat belts it is compulsory to wear them. Failure to do so could result in an on-the-spot fine.

Boats

They may be clichéd but the glass-topped *bateaux-mouches* (also called *vedettes*) that chug up and down the Seine are one of the best ways of seeing Paris. Many of her most famous monuments are visible along the bank: the Eiffel Tower, the Louvre, Notre-Dame Cathedral and the new Musée d'Orsay among them. The cheapest way to do it is the straightforward tour (there is a commentary in English). Some boats also serve tea, or you can pay around ten times as much to have lunch on board, or even more for dinner and a light show.

There are a number of different companies leaving from different points along the Seine. Take the Métro to any one of: Pont Neuf, Alma Marceau, or Bir-Hakeim/Iéna. Boats leave regularly. The tourist office (at the Champs-Elysées, main railway stations, Marie de Paris and the Eiffel Tower – in summer) have brochures and timetables.

Buses

Buses are one way of seeing the city (especially route 24), although traffic can be very heavy. Bus stops show the numbers of the buses that stop there. There is a map of the stops *en route*, and you can get maps of the whole system from

Métro stations, bus terminals and the tourist office. You may also see a ticket machine. Some stops have a ticket machine for queuing, since the French seem to be incapable of standing in a straight line. Take one as soon as you arrive at the stop.

Also, do not forget to ring the bell when you want to get off as the bus will not stop automatically. Buses start at 06.30. Some routes end at around 21.00, others run until 00.30. There are special night buses ('*noctambus*') (you hail them) which run in various directions every hour between 01.30 and 05.30 from the place du Châtelet. A special *Montmartrobus* tours the Montmartre district.

You can also get excursions on the buses to places like Versailles which work out much cheaper than taking one of the sightseeing coach tours. Bus tickets are the same as those for the Métro although they are divided into fare stages. You need one ticket for a journey of one or two fare stages and two or more tickets for three or more fare stages.

Canals

You can take a barge along the canals running through and out of Paris. La Villette and the Cité des Sciences et de l'Industrie is one of the most popular destinations.

Tickets and information are available from:

Canauxrama 13 quai de la Loire, 19e (tel: 42 39 15 00)

Paris Canal 19 quai de la Loire, 19e (tel: 42 40 96 97).

Coach Tours

Several companies offer sightseeing coach tours of the city. Some are double-decker buses with huge glass windows. Commentaries are either through headphones which you set to the language you want or through multi-lingual guides. There are several possibilities, depending on how much time you have to spare, including tours of museums, and visits to nightspots like the Lido which may include a meal. The organised tours are a lot more expensive than making your own arrangements.

You can also buy coach excursions to sites outside Paris including Versailles, Malmaison, Giverny and Chartres. You can make your own way there much cheaper by using public transport (see **Excursions from Paris**, pages 41–44).

For your money you get a guide, and a commentary or piped music on board the bus, although often only a limited amount of time in the place. You should book in advance, either by telephone or by calling into the office in person:

Cityrama, 4 places des Pyramides, ler (tel: 42 60 30 14)
Paris Vision, 214 rue de Rivoli, ler (tel: 42 60 31 25)
Paris Bus departs from the Eiffel Tower (tel: 42 30 55 50).

Métro

The entrances to many of Paris's Métro stations can be spotted in the streets by their distinctive art nouveau designs and huge M signs.

The various lines are numbered and are known by the names of the stations at each end, the

A bus ride can take in the major sites of Paris and be much cheaper than an official coach tour

correspondances are the points at which lines join. Look for signs for the relevant *direction* you are travelling in and follow the colour-coded and numbered lines. Changing Métro lines is quite easy once you get the hang of it.

There are usually large plans of the whole network outside each station, some with illuminated buttons which are fun to operate. A map of the Métro will be found on page 110,

© TCS

and there is also a Métro/RER map on the back of the free map of Paris available from the tourist office.
Outside some stations (numbers increasing daily) there are computerised route finders

called SITU (*systéme d'information de trajets urbains*). You tap in the name of the street you want to get to and get a print-out of the quickest way to get there, including walking. Most stations are quite cheerful

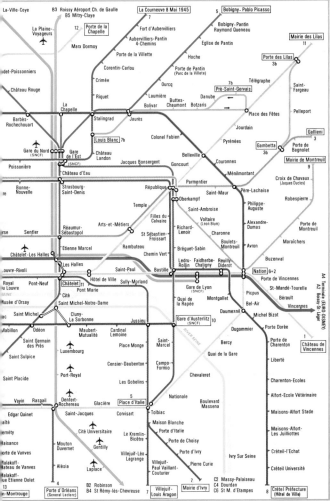

DIRECTORY

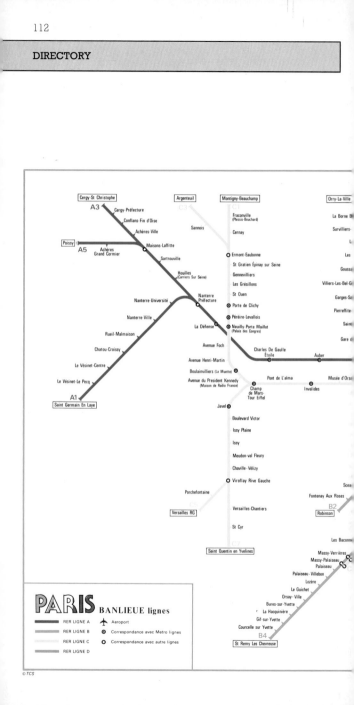

PARIS BANLIEUE lignes

RER LIGNE A
RER LIGNE B
RER LIGNE C
RER LIGNE D

✈ Aeroport
◎ Correspondance avec Metro lignes
○ Correspondance avec autre lignes

© TCS

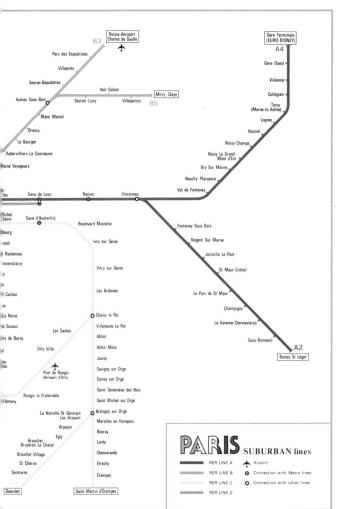

Roissy-Aéroport Charles de Gaulle   B3

Gare Terminale (EURO-DISNEY)   A4

Parc des Expositions

Villepinte

Sevran-Beaudottes

Gare Ouest

Violenne

Collégien

Vert Galant   Mitry - Claye

Aulnay Sous Bois   Sevran-Livry   Villeparisis   B5

Torcy (Marne-la-Vallée)

Blanc Mesnil

Lognes

Drancy

Noisiel

Le Bourget

Noisy-Champs

Aubervilliers-La Courneuve

Noisy Le Grand-Mont d'Est

...aine Voyageurs

Bry Sur Marne

Neuilly - Plaisance

Val de Fontenay

...les   Gare de Lyon   Nation   Vincennes

...Michel ...Dame   Gare d'Austerlitz

...bourg

...oyal

Boulevard Masséna

Fontenay Sous Bois

...it Rochereau

Ivry sur Seine

Nogent Sur Marne

...niversitaire

Joinville Le Pont

...y

St Maur-Créteil

...a

...l- Cachan

Vitry sur Seine

...ux

Le Parc de St Maur

...La Reine

Les Ardoines

Champigny

...e Sceaux

La Varenne-Chennevières

...ix de Berny

...y

Les Saules

Choisy le Roi

Villeneuve Le Roi

Sucy-Bonneuil   A2

Boissy St Léger

Orly Ville

Ablon

...ne ...ion

Athis-Mons

Pont de Rungis (Aéroport d'Orly)

Juvisy

Savigny sur Orge

Rungis la Fraternelle

Épinay sur Orge

Saint Geneviève des Bois

...d'Antony

Saint Michel sur Orge

La Norville St Germain Les Arpajon

Brétigny sur Orge

Marolles en Hurepoix

Arpajon

Bouray

Egly

Lardy

Breuillet Bruyères Le Chatel

Chamarande

Breuillet-Village

Étréchy

St Chéron

Étampes

Sermaise

...C4   ...D3

Dourdan   Saint Martin d'Étampes

PARIS SUBURBAN lines

▬▬▬ RER LINE A   ✈ Airport
▬▬▬ RER LINE B   ◉ Connection with Metro lines
▬▬▬ RER LINE C   ○ Connection with other lines
▬▬▬ RER LINE D

User No. 9C/02/117

DIRECTORY

inside with gaily coloured plastic seats and matching tiles, plus videos to watch to while away the time.

The Louvre station is an extension of the museum, with works of art displayed in cabinets along the platform. There are the usual buskers but in Paris they do it in style, playing jazz and classical music on trains as well as off. Some of them may well be students from the Conservatoire National.

It is forbidden to smoke on the Métro. There is a warning siren just before the doors close, and you release the door yourself if you want to get off.

The first Métro is at 05.30. The last at 00.30. As in most other cities, it is inadvisable to get into an empty carriage alone, especially late at night.

The Paris Métro is fast, clean and efficient. The colour-coded and numbered lines are simple to follow

RER

The RER is the fast suburban service which will take you to places like Versailles (much cheaper than an organised excursion). The lines are divided into sections and the cost of a ticket (you can use the same ones as on the buses or the Métro within the metropolitan area) varies according to the number of sections you cross. The RER goes to Charles-de-Gaulle and Orly airports. (Also see pages 110 and 112.) The main lines are:

Ligne A: Saint-Germain-en-Laye to Boissy-Saint-Léger or Marne-la-Vallée (for Euro Disney)
Ligne B: Saint-Rémy-les-Chevreuse to Gare du Nord to Roissy (airport) or Mitry-Claye
Ligne C: Massy-Palaiseau, Dourdan or St-Martin-d'Etampes to Versailles or St-Quentin-en-Yvelines
Ligne D: Châtelet-les-Halles to Orry-la-Ville

Taxis

Taxis can be hailed if you are lucky enough to see one with both lights on the roof showing. One light means it is occupied. You must not hail a taxi within 20 yards (18m) of a rank or *tête de station*.

All taxis have meters and there are supplements for luggage. Pick-up charges from and to stations and airports are higher than from the nearest street corner.

There are also surcharges after 22.00 and before 06.30, for

heavy luggage and on Sundays. Queues can be vast, especially at the Gare du Nord. You are expected to tip around 10 to 15 per cent. It is sometimes very difficult indeed to get a taxi. Your hotel or restaurant will usually ring for one but even at top hotels like the de Crillon you have to wait outside in a queue like everyone else. Taxis will seldom take more than three people.

You can try to book a cab in advance by telephoning:
G7 Radio: 47 39 47 39
Alpha Taxi: 45 85 85 85
Taxi Bleus: 49 36 10 10
Taxi Radio Etoile: 42 70 41 41
For complaints write to:
Suivis Taxi, Préfecture de Police, 36 rue des Morillons, 75015 Paris.

Tickets

If you are staying only a short while, the cheapest way to travel is to buy a *carnet* or book of ten tickets rather than to buy a ticket for each individual journey. You only need one ticket for each RER or Métro journey regardless of how long it is or how many times you change trains. The same tickets can be used on the buses (see above).

You should buy tickets from the booking office or from *tabacs*, slot machines or bus terminals. A *Paris-Visite* ticket valid for three or five days is worth it only if you plan a lot of travelling. It gives you unlimited travel on the Métro, RER, SNCF suburban services and buses. There are two types of ticket: Paris and nearby suburbs, and Paris and the Ile de France (including Versailles and Orly and Roissy airports). The ticket also gives reductions on a limited number of tourist attractions and services. You can buy them in main Métro stations, at SNCF railway stations, in tourist offices, banks and some hotels, at Orly and Roissy airports and at the RATP sales office at 35 bis quai des Grands Augustins, 6e, or in the place de la Madeleine, 8e. The *Formule 1* ticket gives one day's unlimited travel for a flat fee on the bus, Métro or RER, and on SNCF suburban services. The ticket can cover one, two, three or four zones, or all zones plus the airports.

The best value if you are staying for a week is the *Carte Orange*. You need a coupon to go with it. The *Coupon Jaune* runs from Monday to Sunday night, a *Coupon Orange* runs for a calendar month. You can buy it a week before the beginning of each month. You need a passport photo. Tickets are available on the spot (they take about five minutes to process) from Métro stations, some banks and the tourist office.

● For Métro, RER and bus information telephone: RATP 43 46 14 14

● For suburban trams telephone: SNCF 45 82 50 50.

Electricity
220V. Two round pins is the most common kind of plug and socket arrangement.

Embassies
British Embassy
35 rue du Faubourg-St-Honoré, 8e
Tel: 42 66 91 42
Canadian Embassy
35 avenue Montaigne, 8e
Tel: 47 23 01 01
United States Embassy
2 avenue Gabriel, 8e
Tel: 42 96 12 02

Emergency Telephone Numbers
Ambulance (SAMU) tel: 15
Police tel: 17
Fire tel: 18
24-hour emergency treatment:
Poison Centre tel: 40 37 04 04
Serious burns (adults) tel: 42 34 17 58
Serious burns (children) tel: 43 73 62 54
SOS Dentaire (dental emergencies) tel: 43 37 51 00
SOS Médicin (doctor) tel: 47 07 77 77

Entertainment
For what's on in English tel: 47 20 88 98.
You can get a free copy of the monthly *Paris Sélection* magazine from the tourist office, or buy *Pariscope* or *l'Officiel des Spectacles* weekly (in French) or the rather more expensive *Passion* magazine (in English) published by *Time Out* every two months.
For a listing of Paris annual events, see pages 93–94.
The tourist office publish a booklet *Saisons de Paris* which lists details of events and major exhibitions.

Health
British nationals holding form E111 are expected to pay for any medical treatment, and claim a partial refund from Caissé Primaire d'Assurance-Maladie de Paris, Service de Relations Internationales, 173-175 rue de Barcy, 75586 Paris Cedex 12 (tel: 43 46 12 53). Private medical insurance is essential for visitors from outside the EC.
American Hospital 63 boulevard Victor Hugo, Neuilly, 5 miles (8km) from the centre (tel: 46 41 25 25).
British Hospital 48 rue de Villeirs, Levallois-Perret, 5 miles (8km) from the centre (tel: 47 58 13 12).

Helicopter Trips
Should you want a bird's eye view of Paris contact:
Hélicap Tel: 45 57 75 51
Héli-France Tel: 45 54 95 11
Héli-Inter Tel: 30 37 30 00

Holidays (**Public**)
New Year's Day
Easter Monday
Labour Day – 1 May
VE Day – 8 May
Ascension Day
Whit Monday
Bastille Day – 14 July

Excusez-moi, Monsieur l'agent…
It pays to address any Parisian politely, especially a member of the gendarmerie

Assumption Day – 15 August
All Saints' Day – 1 November
Armistice Day – 11 November
Christmas Day

Information

The main tourist office is at 127 avenue de Champs-Elysées (tel: 47 23 61 72), on the left, at the top just before the Arc de Triomphe. It is open every day from 09.00 to 20.00. They will ring around (for a booking fee) to find a hotel room for you (cancelled if you do not turn up within one and a half hours) and will supply you with brochures, free city and Métro maps and limitless information on the city. There are also tourist offices at the main stations (Gare du Nord, Gare de l'Est, Gare de Lyon, Gare Montparnasse, Gare d'Austerlitz) and at the Eiffel Tower (from 11.00 to 18.00) from

118

DIRECTORY

May until the end of September,
and the Marie de Paris at 29 rue
de Rivoli (from 09.00 to 18.00,
closed Sunday).
Tourist information (in English) is
available round the clock by
phoning: 47 20 88 98.

French Government Tourist Office
Britain 178 Piccadilly, London
W1V 0AL (tel: 071-499 6911).
USA 610 First Avenue, New York,
NY 10020 (tel: 212 757 1125).

Lost Property
Go along to 36 rue des Morillons
15e (Métro: Convention), as
information is not given over the
phone. Open Monday to Friday
08.30 to 17.00 (Tuesday and
Thursday until 20.00).

Money Matters
Banks are open on weekdays
from 09.00 to 16.30. You can
change money at foreign
exchange offices at the airports
and main stations (as well as in
stores like Printemps and
Galeries Lafayette). There is an
automatic exchange machine
(open 24 hours) in the Point-
Show Gallery, Champs-Elysées.
At weekends you can change
money at:
Banco Central, Gare d'Austerlitz
(daily 07.00 to 21.00)
CCF, 117 Champs-Elysées, 8e
(Saturday 08.30 to 20.00)
UBP, 154 Champs-Elysées, 8e
(10.30 to 18.00 at weekends)
CIC, Gare de Lyon (daily 06.30
to 23.00)
CIC, Georges Pompidou Centre
(12.00 to 19.00 daily and from
10.00 to 19.00 on Saturday and
Sunday. Closed Tuesday)
Thomas Cook, Gare du Nord

(daily 06.30 to 22.00, Monday to
Friday)
Thomas Cook, Gare Saint-Lazare
(daily 07.00 to 21.00)

Credit Cards
You can use credit cards in most
hotels and restaurants, but not
usually in small shops, or cafés.
The main numbers for reporting
a loss (24hrs) are:
American Express 47 77 72 00
Diners' Club 47 62 75 00
Eurocard Mastercard 45 67 84
84
Visa and Carte Bleue 42 77 11 90
You should also report the loss to
the nearest police station and
obtain a written statement from
them to support any subsequent
claim.

Tax Refund
It is a bit of a hassle but you can
get a tax refund of 13 to 18 per
cent on goods bought for export
if you shop at a store that is
prepared to deal with the
formalities. Ask if they offer *la
détaxe*. If you come from an EC
country the minimum purchase is
usually 4,200F per article,
outside the EC 2,000F per article.
You have to pay in full and fill in a
form which you then hand into
customs as you leave with a
stamped addressed envelope.
The tax discount will be sent on
to you. There is a special desk on
the main concourse at Orly
airport and on the third floor in
the departure building at
Charles-de-Gaulle airport to deal
with the paperwork.
The amount of tax varies
according to the type of article
bought . The discount of 18 per
cent applies to perfumes, furs,
jewellery and camera equipment.

You can claim for 13 per cent on other articles.

Opening Times
Banks (see **Money Matters**)

Museums
Opening times vary, but national museums (except the Musée d'Orsay, Musée Rodin and Versailles) are closed on Tuesday, while most other city museums are usually closed on Monday.

The Musée d'Orsay on the Left Bank attracted four million visitors in its first year of opening

Post Offices (see **Post Office**)

Shops
Most shops open from 09.00 or 10.00 to 20.00. Some shops shut for lunch between 12.00 and 14.00 and all day on Sunday and Monday. Large department stores open from 09.30 to 18.30 and until 21.00 or 22.00 one or two days a week. Food shops open from Monday or Tuesday to Saturday from 07.00 to 13.30 and again from 16.30 until 20.00. Some are open on Sunday morning until noon.

DIRECTORY

Pharmacies
Recognised by a green cross.
British-American Pharmacy, 1 rue Auber, 9e. English-speaking staff. Open 08.30 to 20.00. Closed Sunday.
Pharmacie Anglaise des Champs-Elysées, 62 avenue des Champs-Elysées, 8e. Stocks English brands. Open until 22.30, closed Sunday.
Pharmacie des Arts, 106 boulevard Montparnasse, 14e. Open until midnight. 09.00 to 13.00 on Sunday.
Pharmacie Dhéry, Galleries des Champs-Elysées, 8e. Open all night, 7 days a week.
Pharmacie Opéra, 6 boulevard des Capucines. Open until 00.30.
Pharmacie Azoulay, 5 place Pigalle. Open until 01.00.
Pharmacie Mozart, 16 avenue Mozart. Open until 22.00. Closed on Sunday.

Places of Worship
There are more than 150 churches and religious buildings in Paris. To find out times and places of services of all denominations contact the Centre International et de Documentation Religieuse, 6 place du Parvis Notre-Dame (tel: 46 33 01 01).
Anglican
Saint George's Church, 7 rue Auguste-Vacquerie, 16e
The American Cathedral, 23 avenue George V, 8e
Buddhist
Temple Bouddhique, 40 route de Ceinture du Lac Daumesnil, 12e
Catholic
Cathédral of Notre-Dame de Paris, 6 Parvis Notre-Dame, 1er
Sacré-Cœur of Montmartre, 36 rue du Chevalier de la Barre, 18e

Saint Joseph's Church, 50 avenue Hoche, 8e
La Madeleine, place de la Madeleine, 8e
French Reformed Church (Protestant)
Poosy l'Annonciation, 10 rue Cortambert, 16e
Temple de l'Oratoire, 147 rue Saint-Honoré, 1er
Jewish
Synagogue, 17 rue St-Georges, 9e
Lutheran
Eglise des Billettes, 24 rue des Archives, 4e
Eglise Baptiste, 48 rue de Lille, 7e
Moslem
Grand Mosquée, 39 rue Geoffroy-St-Hilaire, 5e
Orthodox
Greek Cathedral of Saint-Etienne, 7 rue Georges Bizet, 16e
Russian Cathedral Sainte-Alexandre, 12 rue Daru, 8e

Police
In an emergency dial 17.
Police HQ: 7 boulevard du Palais, 4e. Tel: 42 60 33 32.

Post Office
Stamps can be bought in post offices and at shops with a 'T' (*tabac*) sign displayed.
Post offices (PTT) are open from 08.00 to 19.00, Monday to Friday and from 08.00 to noon on Saturday. The central post office in Paris is at 52 rue du Louvre, 1er (they are open 24 hours a day). They will keep your *poste restante* letters.
The post office at 71 avenue des Champs-Elysées is also open on Sundays and public holidays. Post boxes are oblong, free-standing or in walls and a mustard colour. If you are posting abroad and

La Madeleine

you get a choice of slots look for one saying *départements étrangers*.

Public Transport
See **Domestic Travel**

Restaurants
Most restaurants open from 12.00 until 14.30 for lunch and from 19.00 to 21.30 or 23.00 for dinner, although cafés and brasseries have longer hours and may stay open until as late as 01.00. During the day you can get snacks at *salons de thé*. Many restaurants are shut at weekends. You should book a table for the better known ones. A free guide is available from tourist offices.

Senior Citizens
Whatever your nationality, over-60-year-old women and over-65-year-old men can get discounts

in museums, on public transport and in places of entertainment (up to 50 per cent). Take your passport on arrival to the *Abonnement* office in any of the main railway stations or to the SNCF office which is on the ground floor of the main tourist office at 127 Champs-Elysées, 8e (Métro: George V). They can sell you a Carte Vermeil, valid for a year (from June to May) and currently costs 65F.
If you have not got the *Carte*, show your passport whenever you have to pay an entrance fee. You may find you still get the discount.

Students
Discounts are available to holders of an International Student Identity Card (ISIC) or a Carte Jeunes (for those under 16). At national museums under-18s are admitted free-of-charge, 18 to 25s are half-price.

DIRECTORY

Swimming

Paris has numerous municipal swimming pools as well as a number of private ones. Some of the more popular ones include: The Piscine des Amiraux, 13 rue des Amiraux, built in 1924 and recently renovated.

There is an indoor and outdoor pool in place Paul Verlaine, 13e (the Piscine Buttes-aux-Cailles). Right in the centre of the city there is an indoor Olympic-size pool in a tropical setting at the Nouveau Forum, the Piscine des Halles, 10 rue de la Rotonde, opposite the church of St-Eustache.

The Piscine Keller at 8 rue de

Sunbathers and sightseers on the Left Bank, near the Musée d'Orsay

l'Ingénieur-Robert-Keller, 15e is popular with keen swimmers and the Piscine Jean Taris, 16 rue Thouin has a toddlers pool.

Telephones

In public places look for a PTT sign. There are often public telephones in bars and brasseries as well as kiosks in the street or at stations. In bars the phone may require a *jeton* which you can buy over the counter or there may be a meter and you settle up after the call.

The French also use magnetic telecards (*télécartes*) which you can buy from post offices, cafés, *tabacs*, and railway stations. The French ringing tone is a series of short, regular bleeps. French phone numbers have eight digits, beginning with 4 in Paris (or 3 or 6 in the suburbs). To phone anywhere in France from Paris precede eight digit numbers with 16 (to phone Paris from outside the city first dial 16, wait for the dialling tone, then dial 1 and then the number).
Operator: 13
Directory information (in French): 12
International directory information: 19 33 12 followed by the country code
To telephone abroad, dial 19, wait for the dialling tone, then the country code, then the area code without the first 0, then the number. (The country code for UK is 44; USA and Canada is 1, Australia is 61, New Zealand is 64.)
Incoming calls can be received at phone booths with a blue bell sign. To send a telgram by phone (in English), call 05 33 44 11. There is a minimum of seven words; the address counts as part of the message.

Ticket Agencies
There are numerous ticket agencies in Paris. Most charge 20 to 25 per cent on top of the ticket. Try:
Billetel, 6 boulevard Sebastopol, 4e (tel: 48 04 75 13); or Virgin Mégastore, 52-60 avenue des Champs-Elysées, 8e (tel: 42 56 52 60).
From Tuesday to Saturday, Kiosque Théâtre, 15 place de la

Madeleine, 8e; or RER Châtelet-les-Halles, 1er, sell half-price tickets from 12.30 until 20.00 on the day of the performance. FNAC bookshops sell tickets for music venues.

Time
Central European Time: Greenwich Mean Time (GMT) + 1 hour (summer GMT + 2 hours).

Tipping
Tipping is not necessary in bars and restaurants where service is *compris*, where it is not (*service non compris*) they will add it on for you but the 15 per cent might come as a bit of a shock on top of a fixed-price menu. It is customary to leave your small change on the saucer in a bar or café if you have taken your drink at the counter. Tax and service will be added automatically to hotel bills but you should tip the concierge if he has been helpful. Porters at railway stations have a set price for wheeling luggage around (currently 7.50F). Taxi drivers expect an extra 10 to 15 per cent. It is also customary to tip usherettes in the cinema as this is their only form of income. You should also give a few francs to the guide in a museum if you have been on a tour.

Toilets
Most of the old *pissoirs* have gone, to be replaced by sterile booth-like unisex toilets. In public places you are expected to tip 2F to the attendant. You may be given toilet paper on your way in. Take toilet paper or tissues with you as many toilets in cheaper bars and cafés do not have it.

LANGUAGE

Useful Words and Phrases

The most useful word in the French language is *s'il vous plaît* or please. You will get a lot further using it after every request than if you leave it out. The French may often be rude but they do not like getting a dose of their own medicine. Also useful is a liberal smattering of *excusez-moi* (excuse me) to prefix questions, followed by *monsieur* or *madame*, depending on whom you are talking to.

Drinks

beer/draught une bière/pression
coffee – iced/ un café – glacé/
black/white noir/au lait
decaffeinated décaféiné
fresh orange juice une orange pressée
hot chocolate chocolat chaud
milk lait
mineral water l'eau minérale
tea/lemon tea un thé/au citron
herb tea infusion, tisane
tonic Schweppes
wine – white/red le vin– blanc/rouge
wine list la carte des vins

Eating Out

cheapest fixed price menu menu conseillé
fixed price menu prix fixe
all included service compris (SC) (ie do not tip)
a little more encore un peu
butter le beurre
can I have the bill? l'addition, s'il vous plaît?
cheese fromage
closed...Monday fermeture lundi
dessert les desserts
first course hors d'œuvre
have you got a table? avez-vous une table de libre?

I would like/we would like je voudrais/on voudrait
...to book a table for two ...une table pour deux
second course entrée
medium rare à point
menu la carte
rare saignant
salt sel
self service libre service (le self)
snacks casse-croûte
all day à toute heure
to eat manger
to drink boire
very rare bleu
well done bien cuit
waiter/waitress monsieur/mademoiselle
what do you recommend? qu'est-ce que vous recommandez?
where are the toilets? où sont les toilettes?

Money

bank/exchange banque/bureau de change
can I have a receipt? puis-je avoir un reçu?
can I change travellers' cheques here? puis-je changer des chèques de voyage ici?
cashier la caisse
change la monnaie
do you accept credit cards? acceptez-vous des cartes de crédit?
do you have change? pouvez-vous me faire la monnaie?
how much is it, please? c'est combien, s'il vous plaît?
exchange rate cours de change
money argent
travellers' cheques chèques de voyage

Shopping

cut price clothes dégriffés/soldes permanents/reduits
closed fermeture

how many/much? combien?
one of those un/une de ceux-là
open ouvert
retail vente au détail
sale soldes
shop le magasin
stamps les timbres
tax refund la détaxe
that's enough ça suffit
that is too much c'est trop
that is all c'est tout
this one ceci
that one cela
what do I owe you? combien je vous dois?
wholesale vente en gros

Types of Shop
bakery la boulangerie
butcher la boucherie
cake shop la pâtisserie
chemist la pharmacie
cheese shop la fromagerie
dairy la crémerie
delicatessen charcuterie/traiteur
fish shop la poissonnerie
food shop une alimentation
grocers' une épicerie
hairdresser le coiffeur
post office le bureau de poste
supermarket le supermarché
sweet shop la confiserie
take-away (grocer) le traiteur

Travelling Around
bridge pont
bus autobus
bus stop arrêt
car park un parking
I am going to je vais à …
I need petrol j'ai besoin d'essence
I need … j'ai besoin de …
a ticket to un billet pour
a book of tickets un carnet
a return ticket un aller retour
a single ticket un aller simple
I want to get off je voudrais descendre

information office syndicat d'initiative/office de tourisme
leave me alone laissez-moi tranquille
museum le musée
my car has broken down ma voiture est en panne
oil huile
parking prohibited défense de stationner/stationnement interdit
petrol essence
petrol station poste d'essence
platform quai
plane avion
please direct me to… pour aller à… s'il vous plaît?
railway station la gare
the road for la route pour
ticket office vente de billets
to cross the road traverser la rue
traffic lights les feux
tyres les pneus
underground Métro

Directions
after après
behind derrière
before avant
here ici
in front of devant
left à gauche
near près
opposite en face de
right à droite
straight on tout droit
there là
where? où?
where is? où est?
what time does it arrive? il arrive à quelle heure?
what time does it leave? il part à quelle heure?
where are we on this map? où sommes-nous sur le plan?
where can I find a taxi? où puis-je trouver un taxi?
where is the station? où est la gare?

LANGUAGE

Vocabulary

yes oui
no non
please s'il vous plaît
thank you merci
bad mauvais
big grand
cold froid
condoms preservatifs
day un jour
far loin
goodbye au revoir
good evening bonsoir
good morning bonjour
good night bonne nuit
good bon
hot chaud
later plus tard
month un mois
now maintenant
small petit
today aujourd'hui
under sous
week une semaine
when? quand?
why? pourquoi?
with avec
without sans
yesterday hier

Phrases

at what time? à quelle heure?
call an ambulance appelez une ambulance s'il vous plaît
could you speak more slowly? pouvez-vous parler plus lentement, s'ilvous plaît?
do you speak English? parlez vous anglais?
help! au secours!
how much is this? combien?
I do not understand je ne comprends pas
I need a doctor je voudrais voir un docteur
I want je voudrais
Is there someone here who speaks English? Y a-t-il quelqu'un qui parle anglais ici?

I'm sorry pardon
thank you very much merci beaucoup
where is the nearest police station? où est le post de police le plus proche?

Numbers

one un
two deux
three trois
four quatre
five cinq
six six
seven sept
eight huit
nine neuf
ten dix
first premier (-ière)
second seconde (deuxième)
third troisième
fourth quatrième
fifth cinqième

Days of the Week

Monday lundi
Tuesday mardi
Wednesday mercredi
Thursday jeudi
Friday vendredi
Saturday samedi
Sunday dimanche
festivals/holidays fêtes/jours fériés

Months of the Year

January janvier
February février
March mars
April avril
May mai
June juin
July juillet
August août
September septembre
October octobre
November novembre
December décembre
Christmas Noël
Easter Pâques

INDEX